中国思想文化术语多语种对外翻译
标准化建设项目成果
CHINESE THINKING AND CULTURE
MULTILINGUAL TERMINOLOGY DATABASE

中华源·河南故事
CHINESE CIVILIZATION
Stories from Henan

黄河流域生态保护

ECO-SYSTEM PROTECTION OF THE YELLOW RIVER BASIN

河南省人民政府外事办公室　编

河南大学出版社
HENAN UNIVERSITY PRESS
·郑州·

图书在版编目（CIP）数据

中华源·河南故事．黄河流域生态保护 / 河南省人民政府外事办公室编．－－郑州：河南大学出版社，2022.10
　　ISBN 978-7-5649-5349-2

Ⅰ．①中⋯ Ⅱ．①河⋯ Ⅲ．①地方文化－河南－通俗读物②黄河流域－生态环境保护－通俗读物 Ⅳ．① G127.61-49 ② X321.22-49

中国版本图书馆 CIP 数据核字（2022）第 218193 号

黄河流域生态保护
HUANG HE LIUYU SHENGTAI BAOHU

责任编辑　　陈　炜
责任校对　　陈晓林
封面设计　　翟淼淼
版式设计　　高枫叶
出版发行　　河南大学出版社
　　　　　　　地址：郑州市郑东新区商务外环中华大厦2401号　　邮编：450046
　　　　　　　电话：0371-86059701（营销部）
　　　　　　　　　　0371-86059750（高等教育与职业教育分公司）
　　　　　　　网址：hupress.henu.edu.cn
排　　版　　河南大学出版社设计排版部
印　　刷　　河南博雅彩印有限公司
版　　次　　2022年10月第1版　　　　　印　　次　　2022年10月第1次印刷
开　　本　　710 mm×1010 mm　1/16　　印　　张　　14
字　　数　　248千字　　　　　　　　　定　　价　　72.00元

版权所有，侵权必究
本书如有印装质量问题，请与河南大学出版社营销部联系调换。

"中华源·河南故事"系列丛书编委会

顾　　问	黄友义　杨　平　范大祺
主　　任	梁杰一
副 主 任	卞　科　陈　岩　陈志伟　刁玉华　方启雄　韩国河
	惠　康　焦开举　介晓磊　孔留安　李冰冰　李　俊
	刘炯天　李向前　李　镇　梁留科　刘金锋　马萧林
	牛书成　牛卫国　屈凌波　屈鹏飞　史永庆　田　凯
	万正峰　王建修　王清义　王自文　许二平　杨建伟
	杨玮斌　俞海洛　张改平　张俊峰　张明超　张松文
	赵卫东
主　　编	梁杰一
副 主 编	李冰冰
编　　委	陈国良　陈　玮　丁　锐　高　阳　徐恒振　郑延保
	孙立英　郭　远

中华源·河南故事·黄河流域生态保护

主　　编	王清义
副 主 编	饶明奇　韩福乐（英文）
中文撰稿	张戴炜　秦天真　王晓岗
英文翻译	高　亢　王晓燕　宋　鹏　周艳芳
英文审校	[法] Philippe Gourbesville

The Editorial Committee
Chinese Civilization
Stories from Henan

Consultants	Huang Youyi Yang Ping Fan Daqi
Director	Liang Jieyi
Deputy Directors	Bian Ke Chen Yan Chen Zhiwei Diao Yuhua
	Fang Qixiong Han Guohe Hui Kang Jiao Kaiju
	Jie Xiaolei Kong Liu'an Li Bingbing Li Jun
	Liu Jiongtian Li Xiangqian Li Zhen Liang Liuke
	Liu Jinfeng Ma Xiaolin Niu Shucheng Niu Weiguo
	Qu Lingbo Qu Pengfei Shi Yongqing Tian Kai
	Wan Zhengfeng Wang Jianxiu Wang Qingyi Wang Ziwen
	Xu Erping Yang Jianwei Yang Weibin Yu Hailuo
	Zhang Gaiping Zhang Junfeng Zhang Mingchao
	Zhang Songwen Zhao Weidong
Chief Editor	Liang Jieyi
Deputy Chief Editor	Li Bingbing
Editors	Chen Guoliang Chen Wei Ding Rui Gao Yang
	Xu Hengzhen Zheng Yanbao Sun Liying Guo Yuan

Chinese Civilization
Stories from Henan
Eco-System Protection of the Yellow River Basin

Editor-in-Chief	Wang Qingyi
Associate Editors-in-Chief	Rao Mingqi Han Fule (English Text)
Writers	Zhang Daiwei Qin Tianzhen Wang Xiaogang
Translators	Gao Kang Wang Xiaoyan Song Peng
	Zhou Yanfang
Translation Proofreader	Philippe Gourbesville (FR)

总　序

中国是世界四大文明古国之一，也是世界上唯一的古代文明传统未曾中断的国家。河南省地处中国中东部，是中华文明和中华民族的重要发祥地，在中国五千年的文明史上，河南作为国家政治、经济、文化的中心就长达三千多年。从某种意义上讲，一部河南史就是半部中国史。这里是中华人文始祖黄帝的故乡，是古丝绸之路的东方起点，是少林功夫和陈氏太极的发源地，这里创建了中国历史上最早的都城，镌刻了中国最古老的文字，诞生了中国最初的商业文明。

伴随着新时代的荣光，河南经济社会发展迅速，人民生活水平显著提升，这是河南人民自力更生、艰苦奋斗的历史结果，也是对外开放带来的益处。河南经济社会的发展、人民生活方式的改变都植根于深层次的文化积淀。为了让世界更多地了解河南，让河南更好地走向世界，2018年以来，河南省人民政府外事办公室认真研析了这片古老土地上的历史文化资源和时代风貌，组织各领域权威专家学者，编译了"中华源·河南故事"中外文系列丛书，选取黄河文化、河洛文化、老子、庄子、黄帝、少林功夫、太极拳、中医、汉字、丝绸之路、古都、农业、大运河、文物、陶瓷、青铜器、手工艺、书法、杂技、豫菜、豫剧、脱贫攻坚、空中丝绸之路、航空城、南水北调、中原粮谷、红旗渠、焦裕禄等多个主题，力图以故事的方式向世界展现一个立体、全面、真实的河南。

当今世界，人类文明无论是在物质还是在精神方面都取得了巨大进步，特别是物质的极大丰富，这在古代世界是完全不能想象的。同时，当代人类也面临着许多突出的难题，比如，贫富差距持续扩大，物欲追求奢华无度，个人主义恶性膨胀，社会诚信不断消减，伦理道德每况愈下，人与自然关系日趋紧张，等等。要解决这些难题，不仅需要运用人类今天的智慧和力量，而且需要运用人类历史上积累和储存的智慧和力量。河南历史文化底蕴深厚、包容性强，在今天仍极具现实意义。中原文化蕴含的思想智慧有助于修身养性，推动人类社会进步发展，焦裕禄精神、红旗渠精神所体现的为民爱民、艰苦奋斗的价值取向是构建人类命运共同体的力量源泉。我们期待与读者们一起从河南故事中汲取更多的智慧和力量，共同创造更加美好的未来。

Series Foreword

China is one of the four ancient civilizations in the world, and is also the only country in the world where the ancient civilization has not been interrupted. Located in east-central China, Henan Province is an important cradle for the Chinese nation and Chinese civilization. In the course of the five thousand years of Chinese history, for more than three thousand years it served as the political, economic and cultural center of the country and therefore, as generally accepted, represents half of the history of China. Henan is the native place of Yellow Emperor, the cradle of Chinese culture, the starting point of the ancient Silk Road in the east, and the birthplace of Shaolin Kungfu and Chen-style Taijiquan—typical examples of the world-renowned Chinese martial arts. It was here that the earliest capital city in China was founded, the oldest Chinese characters engraved, and the earliest commerce took shape.

In the new era, Henan has witnessed rapid growth in its economy and remarkable improvement of people's living conditions owing to the national reform and opening-up policy and unremitting endeavors of the people. Modern economic achievements and social development as well as the changes of way of life could be traced back to its traditional values and cultural heritages. To enable people from other countries to understand Henan, and let the Province integrate more efficiently into the world development, the Foreign Affairs Office of the People's Government of Henan Province has organized teams of authoritative experts and scholars in relevant fields to compile this *Chinese Civilization: Stories from Henan* in Chinese and foreign languages since 2018 by crystallizing the excellence of traditions and outstanding features of modern development. The book series include *The Yellow River Culture*, *Heluo Culture*, *Laozi*, *Zhuangzi*, *The Yellow Emperor*, *Shaolin Kungfu*, *Taijiquan*, *Traditional Chinese Medicine*,

Chinese Characters, *The Silk Road*, *Ancient Chinese Capitals*, *Feeding the People—Agriculture*, *The Grand Canal*, *Cultural Heritage*, *Ceramic*, *Bronze*, *Handicraft Art*, *Calligraphy*, *Acrobatics*, *Henan Cuisine*, *Henan Opera*, *Poverty Alleviation*, *Silk Road in the Air*, *Zhengzhou—An Aviation City*, *South-to-North Water Diversion*, *Grain of the Central Plains*, *Man-Made River—Hongqiqu Canal*, *A Model Official—Jiao Yulu*, etc., presenting a panoramic picture of the Province.

In today's world, human civilization has made great progress in both material accumulation and ethical advancement, and the great abundance of materials today, especially, is beyond the imagination of the ancient people. At the same time, however, modern people are also confronted with a lot of problems, such as the widening gap between the rich and the poor, the indulgence in pursuit of luxury and extravagance, the undesirable extension of individualism, the decline of social integrity, and the increasingly tense relationship between man and nature. To solve the problems, we need to draw on the wisdom and powers developed today as well as those accumulated in the past. Henan is endowed with rich historical and cultural heritages characterized by its inclusiveness, and such heritages remain significant today. The intelligence and wisdom in Henan culture are conducive to self-cultivation and to the promotion of social development. The spirit of serving the people and relentless struggle, as embodied in Jiao Yulu and the man-made river—Hongqiqu Canal provides source of strength for building a community with a shared future for mankind. It is our hope that wisdom and strength from Henan stories could lead us to a shared brilliant future.

前　言

"中华源·河南故事"中外文系列丛书是河南省人民政府外事办公室首创的特色品牌，自 2020 年发布以来已经成为河南省对外宣传的文化名片和海外友人感知河南的文化窗口。华北水利水电大学结合办学特色，由校党委书记王清义带队为"中华源·河南故事"注入"水"元素，生动讲好"黄河流域生态保护"，展现造福于民的母亲河形象。

水是生命之源、生产之要、生态之基。作为哺育了万千华夏子民的母亲河，黄河流域的生态保护事关中华民族伟大复兴和永续发展的千秋大计。河南省位于黄河中下游，在黄河全流域生态文明建设中肩负着特殊使命和艰巨任务。2019 年 9 月，习近平总书记在郑州主持召开黄河流域生态保护和高质量发展座谈会并发表重要讲话，提出要坚持生态优先、绿色发展，让黄河成为造福人民的幸福河。2021 年 10 月，中共中央、国务院印发的《黄河流域生态保护和高质量发展规划纲要》为黄河流域生态保护事业提供了制度保障。

编写和翻译本书的主要目的，是向世界宣传黄河水情，分享黄河流域生态保护工作的成就和经验。黄河是中国的，也是世界的。保护黄河流域生态，实现高质量发展，既是中国人民的强烈愿望，也是保护全球生态的重要组成部分，中国政府和人民愿意与其他国家和人民分享中国智慧。

本书的主要内容是介绍黄河流域生态要素及河南境内黄河工程的基本情况，分析水利工程与生态保护的关系，总结黄河流域生态保护工作的成就和经验。本书共分为四部分：第一章"黄河流域概况"，主要介绍黄河河道变迁、流域气候、资源能源、水文水沙、水利资源、生态环境等基本情况。第二章"河南境内典型黄河枢纽工程",主要介绍小浪底水利枢纽、三门峡水利枢纽、故县水库、陆浑水库、西霞院反调节水库、河口村水库、郑州黄河铁路大桥等河南境内黄河上的主要工程情况。第三章"黄河流域水利工程对生态保护的意义",主要论述黄河流域环境变迁、历史上黄河流域的洪涝灾害及防治、黄河流域水利枢纽工程与生态环境、水利工程归根到底是生态工程、建立生态环境良好的黄河流域水利工程体系等。第四章"黄河生态文明",主要论述生态文明思想基本内容、习近平生态文明思想、黄河流域生态保护和修复、气候变化与黄河流域生态保护、黄河生态保护与修复对世界文明的影响等。

  本书的编写过程中,参考了国内外有关学者的研究成果,限于体例,未能一一列举,在此一并表示感谢!限于水平,难免有错误、疏漏、肤浅之处。欢迎广大读者批评指正!

2022 年 5 月

Preface

Chinese Civilization: Stories from Henan is a special book series initiated by the Foreign Affairs office of Henan Provincial Government. Since its release in 2020, it has become a cultural name card for Henan Province to publicize abroad and a window for overseas friends to perceive Henan. In combination with its school running characteristics, North China University of Water Resources and Electric Power, led by Pro. Wang Qingyi, Secretary of the Party Committee of the University, adds rich "water" elements to the series, in which, stories about ecological protection of the Yellow River Basin have been told and a vivid image of the mother river that benefits Chinese people has been displayed.

Water is the source of life, the essence of production and the foundation of ecology. The Yellow River is the mother river that has nurtured thousands of the Chinese people, therefore its ecological protection is crucial to the great rejuvenation and sustainable development of the Chinese nation. Henan Province, located in the middle and lower reaches of the Yellow River, also shoulders a special mission and arduous task in the construction of ecological civilization in the whole Yellow River Basin. In September 2019, President Xi Jinping presided over the symposium on ecological protection and high-quality development of the Yellow River Basin in Zhengzhou and delivered an important speech, proposing to adhere to ecological priority and green development, and make the Yellow River a happy river that benefits Chinese people. In October 2021, *Outline of the Yellow River Basin's Ecological Protection and High-Quality Development Plan* promulgated by the CPC Central Committee and the State Council provided an institutional guarantee for the cause of ecological protection in the Yellow River Basin.

The main purpose of compiling and translating this book is to publicize the water situation of the Yellow River to the world and share the achievements and experience of ecological protection in the Yellow River Basin. The Yellow River belongs to both

China and the world. Protecting the ecology of the Yellow River Basin and achieving high-quality development is not only the strong desire of the Chinese people, but also an important part of protecting the global ecology. The Chinese government and people are willing to share Chinese wisdom with other countries and people.

The main content of this book is to introduce the ecological elements of the Yellow River Basin and the Yellow River projects located in Henan, analyze the relationship between water conservancy projects and ecological protection, and summarize the achievements and experience of ecological protection in the Yellow River Basin in China. The book is divided into four parts: the first chapter is "Overview of the Yellow River Basin", which mainly introduces the basic situation of the Yellow River's channel change, basin climate, resources and energy, hydrology, water and sediment, water resources, and ecological environment. The second chapter is "Typical Yellow River Hydro Projects in Henan", covering Xiaolangdi Water Conservancy Project, Sanmenxia Water Conservancy Project, Guxian Reservoir, Luhun Reservoir, Xixiayuan Counter-Regulation Reservoir, Hekou Village Reservoir, and the Zhengzhou Yellow River Railway Bridge. The third chapter is "Significance of the Yellow River Basin Water Conservancy Project for Ecological Protection", including the environmental changes in the Yellow River Basin, flood control and prevention in the history, water conservancy projects and ecological environment in the Yellow River Basin, the equivalence relation between water conservancy projects and ecological projects, and the establishment of ecology-friendly water conservancy projects. The fourth chapter is "the Yellow River Ecological Civilization", which mainly discusses the ecological civilization thought, including Xi Jinping's Ecological Civilization Thought, the ecological protection and restoration of the Yellow River Basin, climate change and the ecological protection of the Yellow River Basin, and the impact of the ecological protection and restoration of the Yellow River on world civilization.

To compile this book, we have referred to important research results of scholars in the field of water resources both at home and abroad. It's a pity that we can't include all of them in the book. We'd like to extend our great appreciation to all the scholars and researchers in this field and to all the readers. Because of the limited competence, it is inevitable to have some errors or biases. Your correction is highly appreciated.

May, 2022

目　录 Contents

第一章　黄河流域概况　001
 一、河道变迁　002
 二、流域气候　008
 三、资源能源　012
 四、水文水沙　018
 五、水利资源　028
 六、生态环境　032

Chapter 1　Overview of the Yellow River Basin 　001
 Ⅰ. Channel Change　003
 Ⅱ. Basin Climate　009
 Ⅲ. Resources and Energy　013
 Ⅳ. Hydrology and Sand　019
 Ⅴ. Water Resources　029
 Ⅵ. Ecology　033

第二章　河南境内典型黄河枢纽工程　037
 一、小浪底水利枢纽　040
 二、三门峡水利枢纽　044
 三、故县水库　048
 四、陆浑水库　052
 五、西霞院反调节水库　056
 六、河口村水库　060
 七、郑州黄河铁路大桥　064

Chapter 2　Typical Yellow River Hydro Projects in Henan	037
Ⅰ. Xiaolangdi Water Conservancy Project	041
Ⅱ. Sanmenxia Water Conservancy Project	045
Ⅲ. Guxian Reservoir	049
Ⅳ. Luhun Reservoir	053
Ⅴ. Xixiayuan Counter-Regulation Reservoir	057
Ⅵ. Hekou Village Reservoir	061
Ⅶ. The Zhengzhou Yellow River Railway Bridge	065

第三章　黄河流域水利工程对生态保护的意义	069
一、黄河流域环境变迁	070
二、历史上黄河流域的洪涝灾害及防治	084
三、黄河流域水利枢纽工程与生态环境	096
四、水利工程归根到底是生态工程	102
五、建立生态环境良好的黄河流域水利工程体系	108

Chapter 3　Significance of the Yellow River Basin Water Conservancy Project for Ecological Protection	069
I. Environmental Changes in the Yellow River Basin	073
II. The History of the Yellow River Basin Floods and Prevention	085
III. The Yellow River Basin Water Resources Hub Projects and the Ecological Environment	097
IV. Water Conservancy Projects Are Ultimately Ecological Projects	103
V. Establishing an Ecologically Sound Water Conservancy Project System in the Yellow River Basin	109

第四章　黄河生态文明	115
一、生态文明思想概述	116
二、习近平生态文明思想	128
三、黄河流域生态保护和修复	140
四、气候变化与黄河流域生态保护	192
五、黄河生态保护与修复对世界文明的影响	198

Chapter 4　The Yellow River Ecological Civilization	115
I. Overview of Ecological Civilization Thought	117
Ⅱ. Xi Jinping's Ecological Civilization Thought	129
III. The Yellow River Basin Ecological Protection and Restoration	141
IV. Climate Change and Ecological Conservation in the Yellow River Basin	193
V. The Impact of Ecological Protection and Restoration of the Yellow River on World Civilization	199

附录：中国历史年代简表	206
Appendix: A Brief Chronology of Chinese History	206

第一章

黄河流域概况

Chapter 1

Overview of the Yellow River Basin

一、河道变迁

浩浩荡荡绵亘五千年的历史长河中，黄河一直带动着人类文明从萌芽走向茁壮。黄河流域孕育滋养了中华民族血脉，在这里诞生了辉煌璀璨的黄河文明，成为华夏文明浓墨重彩的一笔。黄河亦被中国人敬畏和尊重，尊为包罗万象、广纳百川的"母亲河"。伴随着地质演变，河流侵蚀、夺袭，历经105万年前的中更新世，各独立的湖盆间逐渐连通，构成黄河水系的雏形。在距今10万至1万年间的晚更新世，黄河逐步演变成为从河源到入海口上下贯通的大河。

黄河是当今中国境内第二大长河，全长5464千米，流域面积75.2万平方千米，约占全国陆地面积的8%。黄河发源于青海省的巴颜喀拉山脉，蜿蜒东流，横跨青藏高原、内蒙古高原、黄土高原和华北平原，奔腾不息注入渤海。流经青海、四川、甘肃、宁夏、内蒙古、陕西、山西、河南、山东9省（区），其中青、甘、宁、内蒙古、晋、陕6省（区）的省会（首府）均在黄河流域内，涉及70个地级行政区，398个县级行政区。

据史料记载，公元前770年周平王迁都成周（今洛阳东），下游平原区逐渐得到开发。春秋后期，齐国首先称霸天下，于公元前685年开始，在黄河下游低平处筑堤防洪，开发被河水淤漫的滩地，称之为"齐桓之霸，遏八流以自广"。战国时期，七雄争霸，韩、赵、魏、齐、燕分居黄河下游。

黄河自陕西潼关进入河南省，西起灵宝市，东至台前县，流经三门峡、洛阳、济源、郑州、焦作、新乡、开封、濮阳等8个省辖市28个县（市、区），河道总长711千米，流域面积3.62万平方千米，分别占黄河流域总面积的5.1%、河南省总面积的21.7%；其保护和受益地区涉及河南省13个省辖市105个县（市、区），面积达9.6万平方千米，占全省面积

Ⅰ. Channel Change

Through the five-thousand-year history, with the drive of the Yellow River, human civilization grows from surviving to thriving. The Yellow River Basin nourished the blood of the Chinese nation and gave birth to the brilliant Yellow River civilization, which has become one of the brightest Chinese civilizations. Also, the Yellow River has been loved and respected by the Chinese people, addressed as the all-embracing "Mother River". With the geological evolution, river erosion and river capture, through the Middle Pleistocene 1.05 million years ago, all the separate lake basins connected, forming the rudiment of the Yellow River system. In the Late Pleistocene, 100,000 to 10,000 years ago, the Yellow River gradually evolved into a great river running from source to mouth without cutoff.

名称：《九曲黄河》　　作者：翟红雨

Picture: Thousands of Bends of the Yellow River

Photographer: Zhai Hongyu

组图 1-1 毛乌素沙地历史照片
（美国克拉克探险队 1908 年 11 月摄）

组图 2-1 毛乌素沙地历史照片
（美国克拉克探险队 1908 年 11 月摄）

组图 1-2 毛乌素沙地现在照片
（喻权刚 2019 年 8 月 11 日摄）

组图 2-2 毛乌素沙地现在照片
（喻权刚 2019 年 8 月 11 日摄）

组图 3-1 毛乌素沙地历史照片
（美国克拉克探险队 1908 年 11 月摄）

组图 4-1 毛乌素沙地历史照片
（美国克拉克探险队 1908 年 11 月摄）

组图 3-2 毛乌素沙地现在照片
（喻权刚 2019 年 6 月 17 日摄）

组图 4-2 毛乌素沙地现在照片
（喻权刚 2019 年 7 月 18 日摄）

百年巨变组图（作者：喻权刚）
Pictures: The Century of Change　Photographer: Yu Quangang

The Yellow River is the second longest river in China, 5,464 kilometers long. The basin covers an area of 752 thousand square kilometers, occupying around 8% of the land area of China. It has the source in the Bayan Har Mountains in Qinghai Province, China, meandering eastward, crossing the Qinghai–Tibet Plateau, Inner Mongolia Plateau, the Loess Plateau, and the North China Plain, finally pouring into the Bohai Sea. The Yellow River flows through nine provinces (provincial districts) including Qinghai, Sichuan, Gansu, Ningxia, Inner Mongolia, Shaanxi, Shanxi, Henan, and Shandong, among which the provincial capitals of Qinghai, Gansu, Ningxia, Inner Mongolia, Shanxi, Shaanxi are all in the Yellow River Basin, totally involving 70 prefecture-level districts and 398 county-level districts.

According to historical records, in the 770 B.C. King Ping of Zhou moved the capital to Cheng Zhou (east of today's Luoyang), the downstream plains exploited gradually. In the late Spring and Autumn period, the state of Qi dominated the world at first, and built embankments since 685 B.C. to prevent floods in the lower reaches of the Yellow River, and exploited the flooded beach. It was said the ruler of Qi prevented the eight streams from spreading. In the Warring States period, seven powerful states were struggling for hegemony, five of which were all located in the downstream of the Yellow River.

The Yellow River enters Henan Province from Tongguan, Shaanxi Province, starting from Lingbao City in the west, reaching Taiqian County in the east, flowing by 28 counties of 8 provincial cities including Sanmenxia, Luoyang, Jiyuan, Zhengzhou, Jiaozuo, Xinxiang, Kaifeng, and Puyang. The total length of the river in Henan is 711 kilometers, and the drainage area is 36,200 square kilometers, accounting for 5.1% of the total area of the Yellow River Basin and 21.7% of the total area of Henan Province. There are 105 counties (cities and districts) in 13 provincial cities in Henan Province benefiting from the Yellow River with an area of 96,000 square kilometers, accounting for 57% of the whole province. The riverbed becomes gentle in the midstream and downstream, and the sediment accumulates, for which the river bank rises year by year. Therefore, the Yellow River is known as a hanging river on the ground.

With time passing by, nowadays over 420 million people live in the

的57%。黄河进入中下游，河床平缓，泥沙淤积，河堤逐年提高，素有"地上悬河"之说。

岁月变迁，直至今日黄河流域已覆盖人口多达4.2亿，约占全国总人口的30.3%，人口分布总体趋势是西北稀东南密，即人口密度呈现出下游＞中游＞上游的排列特性。这条哺育了万千华夏子民的母亲河，正在以它宽广包容的博大胸怀，滋养越来越多后世人享用其福泽硕果。

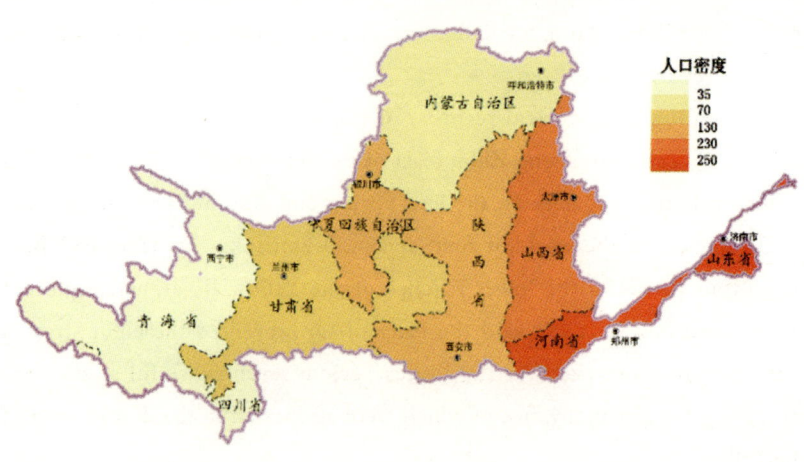

黄河流域人口密度空间分布
Spatial Distribution of Population Density in the Yellow River Basin

Yellow River Basin, occupying almost 30.3% of China's population. Generally speaking, it is sparsely populated in the northwest while densely populated in the southeast. In other words, the population density presents the characteristic of decreasing progressively from downstream, midstream to upstream. The mother river which feeds the Chinese people is nourishing more and more people with its broad mind.

二、流域气候

　　黄河流域东临渤海,西起内陆,大体位于中国中北部,属大陆性气候,各地气候条件差异鲜明,东南部基本属半湿润气候,水草丰茂风调雨顺;中部属半干旱气候,中原广袤四季更迭;西北部为干旱气候,塞外驼铃千里风情。流域年平均气温6.4℃,由南向北、由东向西递减。近20年来,随着全球气候变暖,黄河流域的气温也升高了1℃左右。

　　根据系列统计,流域多年平均年降水量446毫米左右。降水量总趋势由东南向西北递减,其中东南部湿润、半湿润流域地区降水量最多,如秦岭、伏牛山及泰山一带,年降水量往往超过800毫米;降水量最少的是流域北部的干旱地区,如宁蒙河套平原年降水量只有200毫米左右。流域降水量的年内分配极不均匀,连续最大4个月降水量占年降水量的68.3%。流域降水量年际变化悬殊,湿润区与半湿润区最大与最小年降水量的比值大都在3以上,干旱、半干旱区最大与最小年降水量的比值

名称:《黄河中下游分界碑》　　　　作者:张 森

Picture: The Middle and Lower Reaches Boundary Monument of the Yellow River
Photographer: Zhang Sen

II. Basin Climate

The Yellow River Basin borders Bohai Sea in the east while originates from inland in the west, most of which is in the north central part of China. Therefore it has a continental type of climate with distinct differences from one region to another. In the southeast region, it has a semi-humid climate with abundant water and good rainfall. In the central region, it has a semi-arid climate with four distinct seasons. In the northwest region, it has an arid climate with vast desert and clustered camels. The average annual temperature of the basin is 6.4 ℃, decreasing from south to north and from east to west. During the past 20 years, the temperature of the Yellow River Basin has risen about 1℃ influenced by global warming.

According to the statistics, the average annual precipitation of the basin has been about 446mm. And the precipitation descends from southeast to northwest. For the humid and sub-humid areas in the southeast, the precipitation is the most, such as Qinling, Funiushan Mountain and Mount Tai areas with the annual precipitation of over 800mm. While for the arid area in the north, the precipitation is the least, such as the Ningmeng Hetao Plain with the annual precipitation of less than 200mm. Besides, the precipitation of the basin within a year is extremely uneven. The maximum precipitation for four consecutive months accounts for 68.3% of the annual precipitation. And the annual precipitation in the basin varies from year to year. The ratio of maximum annual precipitation to minimum in humid and sub-humid areas is mostly above 3 times, while the ratio of that in arid and sub-arid areas is generally 2.5 to 7.5 times.

The water surface evaporation in the Yellow River Basin varies greatly with temperature, topography, geographical location, etc. The temperature in Lanzhou City and its northern areas is lower with the average water surface evaporation of 790mm. The climate between Lanzhou City and Hekou Town is very dry with a small amount of precipitation, and there are many deserts and arid grasslands. Thus, the average water surface evaporation there reaches 1360mm. In addition, the average water surface evaporation between Hekou Town and Huayuankou District is about 1070mm, and that in the southern areas of Huayuankou District is 990mm.

一般在 2.5 ~ 7.5 之间。

　　黄河流域水面蒸发量随气温、地形、地理位置等变化较大。兰州以上气温较低，平均水面蒸发量 790 毫米；兰州至河口镇区间，气候干燥，降雨量少，多沙漠干旱草原，平均水面蒸发量 1360 毫米；河口镇至花园口区间平均水面蒸发量约 1070 毫米；花园口以下平均水面蒸发量 990 毫米。

　　黄河有着南北鲜明的差异，也有着纵横东西的风采，正因其气象万千的瑰丽，这条河才更有令人折服的魅力。它的大气磅礴，也正是中国万里山河绵亘无垠最好的彰显。

The Yellow River has distinct differences between the south and the north while it shows charming from the east to the west. It is precisely because of its variety that this river is even more attractive. The magnificence of the Yellow River also best manifests the vast territory of China.

三、资源能源

1. 土地资源

黄河流域总土地面积11.9亿亩（含内流区），占全国国土面积的8.3%，其中大部分为山地和丘陵，分别占流域总面积的40%和35%，平原仅占17%。由于地貌、气候和土壤的差异，形成了复杂多样的土地利用类型，不同地区土地利用情况差异很大。

流域内现有耕地2.44亿亩，农村人均耕地3.5亩，约为全国农村人均耕地面积的1.4倍。流域内大部分地区光热资源充足，生产发展尚有很大潜力。流域内现有林地1.53亿亩，牧草地4.19亿亩，林地主要分布在中下游，牧草地主要分布在上中游，林牧业发展前景广阔。

名称：《黄河岸边丰收歌》　　　　　　　　　　作者：崔莉

Picture: The Harvest along the Yellow River
Photographer: Cui Li

2. 矿产资源

黄河流域矿产资源丰富，已探明的矿产有114种之多，在全国已探明的45种主要矿产中，黄河流域就有37种，可谓是地大物博积淀深厚。

III. Resources and Energy

1. Land Resources

The total land area of the Yellow River Basin is 1.19 billion *mu* (including the endorheic areas), almost 8.3% of the national land area, and most of the lands are taken up by mountains and hills which account for 40% and 35% of the total drainage area respectively, while the plain just accounts for 17%. Due to the differences of landform, climate and soil in different regions, lands are utilized in complex and diverse ways, thus the situations of land use in different regions are very different.

The cultivated land in the Yellow River Basin covers 244 million *mu*, and the per capita cultivated land area of rural area is 3.5 *mu*, about 1.4 times as much as that of the whole country. With sufficient light and heat resources, most regions in the basin are potential places for production and development. The forestry and animal husbandry has a broad prospect with 153 million *mu* woodlands distributed in the middle and downstream and 419 million *mu* grasslands in the upper and middle stream.

2. Mineral Resources

The Yellow River Basin is rich in mineral resources with 114 kinds of detected minerals, 37 of which are the major mineral resources while there are about 45 kinds in the whole country totally. It can be said that the Yellow River Basin is an area embracing vast territory and abundant resources. Also, it is particularly rich in mineral reserves of coal, rare earth, gypsum, quartzite for glass, niobium, bauxite, molybdenum, and refractory clay and so on, much richer than those in other regions. In addition to this, there are regionally advantageous minerals like petroleum, natural gas, sodium sulfate, trona, pyrite, limestone for cement, tungsten, copper, rock gold and so on. All these come from the particular ore formation conditions. The mineral reserves are distributed broadly and intensively, which creates favorable conditions for long-term exploitation. There are 10 resource concentration areas such as Xinghai-Maqin-Diebu area, Xining-Lanzhou area, Lingwu-Tongxin-Shizuishan area, Hetao area in Inner Mongolia,

煤、稀土、石膏、玻璃用石英岩、铌、铝土矿、钼、耐火黏土等 8 种矿产储量尤其丰富，在全国范围内优势明显；除此之外还有诸多具有地区性优势的矿物，诸如石油、天然气、芒硝、天然碱、硫铁矿、水泥用灰岩、钨、铜、岩金等。这一切都得益于黄河流域内丰富多样的成矿条件，矿产资源既分布广泛又相对集中，为开发利用等长远规划提供了有利条件。流域内有兴海-玛沁-迭部区、西宁-兰州区、灵武-同心-石嘴山区、内蒙古河套地区、晋陕蒙接壤地区、陇东地区、晋中南地区、渭北区、豫西-焦作区及下游地区等 10 个资源集中区，形成了各具特色和不同规模的生产基地，进行集约化开采利用。除此之外，流域内还有矿产成分复杂的有色金属，共生、伴生多种有益成分，综合开发利用潜力极大。

3. 能源资源

黄河流域煤炭、石油、天然气和有色金属资源丰富，煤炭储量占全国的 50% 以上，水能资源在中国七大江河中居第二位，是中国重要的能源、化工、原材料和基础工业基地，被称为"能源流域"。在全国已探明储量超过 100 亿吨的 26 个煤田中，黄河流域有 12 个，如内蒙古鄂尔多斯、晋中和晋东、陕北、宁东、豫西、陇东等能源基地。流域内已探明的石油、天然气储量分别为 90 亿吨和 2 万亿立方米，分别占全国总地质储量的 40% 和 9%，主要分布在胜利、中原、长庆和延长 4 个油区，其中胜利油田是中国的第二大油田。

正所谓一方水土养一方人，而黄河流域以其纵横万里的广阔胸襟，时时刻刻在燃烧自己支援华夏建设。它像一位积淀多年沉稳慈祥的智者，给我们带来丰富的资源与无穷的智慧，而我们也必将站在黄河这一巨人的肩头更高远眺，迈向一个又一个更加灿烂的辉煌。

contiguous area of Shanxi, Shaanxi and Inner Mongolia, eastern Gansu area, central and southern Shanxi, northern Shaanxi, western Henan-Jiaozuo area and some downstream areas, and so on, which formed production bases with different characteristics and scales for the intensive exploitation. Besides, it is promising to develop and exploit the basin as there are nonferrous metals with complex mineral composition and other profitable materials along with them.

名称：《如火如荼》　　　　　　　　　　　　　　作者：杜建中

Picture: Busy for the Construction
Photographer: Du Jianzhong

3. Energy Resources

The Yellow River Basin is abundant in coal, petroleum, natural gas and nonferrous metals with coal reserves taking up over 50% of the national total and hydro-power resources ranking second in the top seven rivers in China. It is called "the Energy Basin", being a base for energy, chemical industry, raw materials and basic industries. Among the 26 coal fields with reserves of more than 10 billion tons in China, there are 12 in the basin, such as the energy base in Ordos, Inner Mongolia, central and eastern parts in Shanxi Province, northern part in Shaanxi Province, eastern part of Ningxia Province, western part in Henan Province,

黄河流域能源基地分布情况
Distribution of Energy Bases in the Yellow River Basin

eastern part in Gansu Province and so on. The detected reserves of petroleum and natural gas are about 9 billion tons and 2,000 billion cubic meters, accounting for 40% and 9% of the county's total respectively. They mainly distribute in Shengli, Zhongyuan, Changqing and Yanchang oil fields, among which Shengli oil field is the second largest in China.

As the saying goes, "People from different regions carry their distinctive characters", the Yellow River Basin is broad and generous enough to support the construction of China like a candle burning itself selflessly. It has brought us rich resources and endless inspiration like a wise and experienced man. We will certainly gain a brighter future standing on the shoulder of the giant—the Yellow River.

四、水文水沙

1. 洪水

说到黄河洪水，按成因可分为暴雨洪水和冰凌洪水两种类型。暴雨洪水主要来自上游和中游，多发生在6—10月。上游洪水主要来自兰州以上地区，中游暴雨洪水来自河口镇至龙门区间、龙门至三门峡区间和三门峡至花园口区间（分别简称河龙间、龙三间和三花间）。冰凌洪水主要发生在宁蒙河段、黄河下游，发生的时间分别在3月、2月。

（1）暴雨洪水

黄河暴雨洪水的开始日期一般是南早北迟，东早西迟。由于流域面积广阔，形成暴雨的天气条件有所不同，上、中、下游的大暴雨与特大暴雨多不同时发生。

黄河上游多为强连阴雨，一般以7月、9月出现概率较大，8月出现概率较小。降雨特点是面积大、历时长、强度不大，主要降雨中心地带为积石山坡。

黄河中游暴雨频繁、强度大、历时短，洪水具有洪峰高、历时短、陡涨陡落的特点。

黄河的下游洪水主要来自中游，中游是下游的主要致灾洪源。由于上游洪水流经区域广袤，加之河道的调蓄作用强劲，再加上宁夏、内蒙古灌区耗水作用，洪水传播至黄河下游后，形成洪水的基流概率也会成倍增加。

Ⅳ. Hydrology and Sand

1. Flood

When it comes to the flood of the Yellow River, it is generally classified into two types according to the cause of its formation: rainstorm flood and ice flood. Rainstorm flood mainly comes from the upper and middle stream, and mostly happens from June to October. Upstream flood mainly comes from regions above Lanzhou on the map, midstream storm flood comes from regions ranging from Hekou Town to Longmen, Longmen to Sanmenxia as well as Sanmenxia to Huayuankou (abbreviated respectively as He-Long area, Long-San area and San-Hua area, which takes the initial letter of each of the two cities or districts, and same rules are applied in the following parts). Ice flood comes from Ningmeng river section, the downstream of the Yellow River, and mostly happens in February to March.

（1）Rainstorm Flood

Talking about the starting time of rainstorm flood in the Yellow River, the south usually comes earlier than the north and the east comes earlier than the west. Considering the wide basin area as well as various weather conditions that form the rainstorm, the heavy rainstorms as well as extremely heavy rainstorms in the upper, middle and lower reaches often occur at a different time.

The upper stream of the Yellow River tends to face the continuously cloudy or rainy weather, frequently in July and September and seldom in August. The rainfall usually covers a large area, lasts a long time and is with low intensity, choosing the stony hillside as its center.

The middle stream frequently encounters heavy rainstorm with large intensity and short duration and floods are characterized by high peaks, short duration and steep rises and falls.

Floods in the lower stream of the Yellow River mainly come from the middle stream, which are the main source of floods in the lower stream. Because the upper stream flood flows through a vast area, along with the strong regulation and storage effect of the river as well as the water consumption effect of irrigation areas in Ningxia and Inner Mongolia, the probability of forming the base flow of

Picture: The Colorful Hukou Waterfalls of the Yellow River
Photographer: Meng Qingjun

（2）冰凌洪水

冰凌洪水主要发生在上游的宁蒙河段，特别是内蒙古三盛公以下河段和下游的山东河段。由于两河段均为自低纬度流向高纬度，在严冬季节，易形成冰凌洪水灾害。

在封河和稳封阶段，由于冰塞壅水造成槽蓄水量增加，河道水位急剧升高，可能导致河水漫溢、堤防决口；在开河阶段由于槽蓄水量沿程释放，形成冰凌洪水，同时由于上游段开河时下游段还未达到自然开河条件，冰盖以下的过流能力不足，容易形成冰塞、冰坝，导致河道水位急剧上涨，威胁堤防安全，甚至造成堤防决口。

冰凌洪水发生在河道解冻开河期间，宁蒙河段解冻开河一般在3月中下旬，少数年份在4月上旬；黄河下游解冻开河一般在2月上中旬，少数年份在3月上旬。冰凌洪水凌峰流量一般为1000～2000m^3/s，实测最大值不超过4000m^3/s。

the flood will also be doubled after the flood spreads to the lower reaches of the Yellow River.

(2) Ice Flood

Ice flood mainly occurs in the upper stream of the Ningmeng river section, especially the lower stream of Sanshenggong in Inner Mongolia and the Shandong section in the lower stream. Since both river sections flow from low latitude to high latitude, causing the ice flooding disaster easily in severe winter.

During the river closure and stable closure stage, the water storage capacity of the trough increases due to ice blockage and backwater, and the water level of the river channel rises sharply, which may lead to overflow of river water and breach of embankments. During the breakup of the ice, the stored water in the trough rushes out, forming the ice flood, besides, since the lower stream section has not yet reached the natural ice breakup condition when the waterway in the upper stream section is opened up, so the flow capacity under the ice sheet is insufficient, easily forming ice plugs and ice dams, causing a sharp rise of the water level, threatening the safety of the embankment, and even causing the embankment to burst.

Ice flood occurs during the thawing and opening of the river. The thawing and opening of the river in the Ningmeng river section happens generally in the middle and late March, and rarely happens in early April; The thawing and opening of the lower reaches of the Yellow River generally happens in the first half of February, and sometimes in early March. The peak flow of ice flood is generally $1,000-2,000 m^3/s$, and the measured maximum is not more than $4,000 m^3/s$.

The ice flood has the following characteristics: firstly, the peak flow is low, but the water level is high. The ice in the river channel increases the flow resistance and reduces the flow velocity, also, the ice blocks the dam, causing the water level of the river channel much higher than that in the ice-free period. Sometimes, the water level may even exceed the historic high. Secondly, the water storage of the river channel is gradually released, causing the peak flow to increase along the way.

冰凌洪水具有以下特点：一是凌峰流量虽小，但水位高。由于河道中的冰凌使水流阻力增大、流速减小，特别是卡冰结坝壅水，使河道水位壅高，同流量水位远高于无冰期，甚至超过伏汛期历年最高洪水位。二是河道槽蓄水量逐步释放，凌峰流量沿程递增。

2. 泥沙及水沙变化

（1）泥沙

黄河是世界上输沙量最大、含沙量最高的河流。从 1919 至 1960 年，人类活动影响较小，基本可代表天然情况，三门峡站实测多年数据显示，其平均输沙量约 16 亿吨，其中粗泥沙（d>0.05mm）约占总沙量的 21%，其淤积量约为下游河道总淤积量的 50%。黄河泥沙的主要特点如下：

一是输沙量大，水流含沙量高。三门峡站多年平均天然含沙量 35kg/m³，实测最大含沙量 911kg/m³（1977 年），均为大江大河之最。

二是地区分布不均，水沙异源。泥沙主要来自中游的河口镇至三门峡区间，来沙量占全河的 89.1%，来水量仅占全河的 28%；河口镇以上来水量占全河的 62%，来沙量仅占 8.6%。

三是年内分配集中，年际变化大。黄河泥沙年内分配极不均匀，汛期 7—10 月来沙量约占全年来沙量的 90%，且主要集中在汛期的几场暴雨洪水。黄河来沙的年际变化很大，实测最大沙量（1933 年陕县站）为 39.1 亿吨，实测最小沙量（2008 年三门峡站）为 1.3 亿吨，年际变化悬殊，最大年输沙量为最小年输沙量的 30 倍。

（2）水沙变化

由于降雨因素和人类活动对下垫面的影响，以及经济社会的快速发展、工农业生产和城乡生活用水大幅度增加，河道内水量明显减少，加上水库工程的调蓄作用，黄河水沙关系发生了明显的变化。

一是来水来沙量明显减少。头道拐、花园口站 1990—2007 年实测

名称：《冰是睡着的水》　　　　　　　　　　　作者：张宝森

Picture: Ice is Frozen Water
Photographer: Zhang Baosen

2. Sediment and Water-Sand Changes

（1）Sediment

The Yellow River ranks the top in the world in terms of sand transport and sand content. Due to the low impact of human activities from 1919 to 1960, the following data can basically reflect the Yellow River conditions in natural state. The data measured by Sanmenxia Station for many years shows that its average sediment transport is about 1.6 billion tons, of which coarse sediment (d>0.05mm) accounts for about 21% of the total sediment, and its siltation is about 50% of the total siltation of the downstream river. The main characteristics of the Yellow River sediment are as follows:

First, the amount of sediment runoff is large due to high sediment content in the water flow. The average sediment content at natural state of Sanmenxia Station for many years is 35kg/m^3, and the measured maximum sediment content is 911kg/m^3 (in 1977), both of which are the highest in large rivers.

平均年来水量分别为 148.7 亿立方米、244.2 亿立方米，比 1950—1989 年实测平均值分别减少 40.0%、45.3%。由于中游降雨量减少、暴雨洪水强度减弱、发生频次减少，以及水利水保措施的作用，三门峡站 1990—2007 年实测输沙量为 6.0 亿吨，比 1919—1960 年实测平均值 16 亿吨减少了约 10 亿吨。

二是径流年内分配发生了明显变化。以 1919—1960 年为例，头道拐、花园口站的实测汛期来水比例分别为 62.1% 和 61.5%。自 1986 年以来，由于龙羊峡、刘家峡等大型水库的调蓄作用和工农业用水的影响，头道拐、花园口站的汛期来水比例分别下降至 38.2% 和 44.0%。

三是汛期有利于输沙的大流量历时和水量减少。1986 年前，潼关站多年平均汛期日均流量大于 3000m^3/s 流量级的历时、相应水量分别为 29.8 天、104.0 亿立方米，1987—2007 年分别减少到 3.4 天、10.6 亿立方米，水流的输沙动力大大减弱。

名称：《绿与黄》　　　　　　　　　　　　　　　作者：崔　鹏

Picture: Green Plants and the Yellow River
Photographer: Cui Peng

Second, the regional distribution is uneven so that the water and sediment are from different sources. The sediment mainly comes from Hekou Town to Sanmenxia City in the middle stream, and the incoming sediment accounts for 89.1% of the whole river while the water only accounts for 28% of the whole. The water inflow above Hekou Town accounts for 62% of the whole river while the sediment inflow only accounts for 8.6%.

Third, the sediment distribution of the Yellow River is extremely uneven throughout the year and the situation differs a lot from one year to another for the period during July to October in the flood season contributes 90% of the sediment volume in the whole year, mainly by several rainstorms and floods in the flood season. The interannual variation of sediment from the Yellow River is great since the measured maximum sediment discharge is 3.91 billion tons (in Shan County Station in 1933) while the minimum is 0.13 billion tons (in Sanmenxia Station in 2008) and the former is 30 times as much as the latter.

(2) Changes of Water and Sediment

The water volume in the river channel has been significantly reduced due to the influence of rainfall and human activities on the underlying surface, rapid development of economy and society, industrial and agricultural production as well as substantial increase of urban and rural domestic water. Coupled with the regulation and storage effect of the reservoir project, the obvious changes have taken place in the water-sediment relationship of the Yellow River.

First, the amount of incoming water and sediment decreased significantly. The measured average annual water volume of Toudaoguai and Huayuankou stations in the year 1990 to 2007 is 14.87 billion cubic meters and 24.42 billion cubic meters respectively, which is 40.0% and 45.3% less than the measured average value in the year 1950 to 1989. Due to the reduction of rainfall in the middle stream, the weakening of rainstorm and flood intensity, the reduction of occurrence frequency, and the effect of water conservancy and soil conservation measures, the measured sediment discharge of Sanmenxia Station in 1990 to 2007 is 0.6 billion tons, about 1 billion tons less than the average value measured from 1919 to 1960.

Second, the annual distribution of runoff has changed significantly. Taking 1919 to 1960 as an example, the measured inflow ratios in the flood season at

四是水沙关系仍不协调。水沙关系不协调是黄河的基本特性，自1986年以来，虽然来沙量有所减少，但由于黄河水量尤其是汛期水量大量减少，使有利于输沙的大流量历时减少、单位流量含沙量增加，水沙关系仍不协调。

即便泥沙与水沙变化为治理黄河带来重重困难，但勤劳智慧的中国人民却从不畏惧，用一次次抗洪胜利来鼓舞信心，用一次次防灾减灾技术进步来造福民生。相信黄河必将成为造福人民的幸福河，这条陪伴我们走过历史春秋的母亲河，也终将向我们展露其最温柔贤淑的一面。

Toudaoguai and Huayuankou stations were 62.1% and 61.5% respectively. Since 1986, due to the regulation and storage of large reservoirs such as Longyangxia and Liujiaxia and the influence of industrial and agricultural water use, the proportion of water inflow at Toudaoguai and Huayuankou stations in the flood season has dropped to 38.2% and 44.0% respectively.

Third, the flood season is conducive to the reduction of large flow duration and water volume in the sediment transport. Before 1986, the duration and corresponding water volume of Tongguan Station with average daily discharge of more than 3,000m^3/s in flood season were 29.8 days and 10.40 billion cubic meters respectively for many years in the flood season. From 1987 to 2007, it reduced to 3.4 days and 1.06 billion cubic meters respectively, causing the sediment transport power of water flow to be greatly weakened.

Fourth, the relationship between water and sediment is still uncoordinated. The disharmonious relationship between water and sediment is the basic characteristic of the Yellow River. Since 1986, although the sediment inflow has decreased, the relationship between water and sediment is still disharmonious because the water volume of the Yellow River, especially the water volume in flood season, has decreased significantly, resulting in the reduction of the duration of large flow conducive to sediment transport and the increase of sediment concentration per unit of the flow.

Even though the changes of sediment and water bring many challenges to the governance of the Yellow River, the hardworking and wise Chinese people have never been frightened. We are inspired by one victory after another of flood fighting and use the disaster prevention and mitigation technology to benefit people's livelihood. We believe that the Yellow River will benefit people and bring happiness to people. This mother river that has accompanied us throughout the long history will eventually show us its tenderest and the most virtuous side.

五、水利资源

根据多年系列水资源调查评价，黄河流域水资源总量为 647.0 亿立方米。其中，现状下垫面条件下的利津站多年平均河川天然径流量 534.8 亿立方米，流域地下水与地表水之间不重复计算量为 112.21 亿立方米。

1. 河川径流

黄河流域河川径流的主要特点如下：

一是水资源贫乏。黄河流域面积占全国国土面积的 8.3%，而年径流量只占全国的 2%。流域内人均水量 473 立方米，仅为全国人均水量的 23%；耕地亩均水量 220 立方米，仅为全国耕地亩均水量的 15%。实际上考虑向流域外供水后，人均、亩均占有水资源量更少。

二是径流年内、年际变化大。干流及主要支流汛期 7—10 月径流量占全年的 60% 以上，支流的汛期径流主要以洪水形式形成，非汛期 11 月至次年 6 月来水不足 40%。干流断面最大年径流量一般为最小值的 3.1—3.5 倍，支流一般达 5—12 倍。

三是地区分布不均。黄河河川径流大部分来自兰州以上，年径流量占全河的 61.7%，而流域面积仅占全河的 28%；龙门至三门峡区间的流域面积占全河的 24%，年径流量占全河的 19.4%。兰州至河口镇区间产流很少，河道蒸发渗漏强烈，流域面积占全河的 20.6%，年径流量仅占全河的 0.3%。

2. 地下水资源

1980—2000 年黄河流域多年平均地下水资源量（矿化度小于等于 2g/L）为 376.0 亿立方米，其中山丘区地下水资源量为 263.3 亿立方米，

V. Water Resources

According to the investigation and evaluation of water resources for many years, the total amount of water resources in the Yellow River Basin is 64.70 billion cubic meters. Among them, the annual average natural runoff of Lijin Station under the current underlying surface condition is 53.48 billion cubic meters, and the non-repeated calculation between groundwater and surface water in the basin is 11.221 billion cubic meters.

1. River Runoff

The main characteristics of river runoff in the Yellow River Basin are as follows:

First, the Yellow River is confronted with water shortage. The area of the Yellow River Basin accounts for 8.3% of the national land area, while the annual runoff accounts for only 2%. When it comes to the water volume per capita, the basin has only 473 m^3, equivalent to 23% of the whole country; The average water volume per *mu* of cultivated land is 220m^3, which is only 15% as much as that in the country. In fact, the water resources per capita and per mu are less if the water supply outside the basin is taken into consideration.

Second, the runoff changes greatly within the year and between years. The runoff of the main stream and main tributaries in the flood season from July to October accounts for more than 60% of the whole year, which comes into being mainly in the form of flood, and the water inflow from November to June of the next year is less than 40% of the whole year in the non-flood season. The maximum annual runoff of the main stream section is generally 3.1 to 3.5 times the minimum value, and that of the tributaries is generally 5 to 12 times.

Third, the regional distribution is uneven. Most of the runoff of the Yellow River comes from above Lanzhou on the map, and the annual runoff accounts for 61.7% of the whole river, while the drainage area only accounts for 28%; The drainage area from Longmen to Sanmenxia accounts for 24% of the whole river, and the annual runoff accounts for 19.4%. The runoff produced from Lanzhou to Hekou Town is limited, and the evaporation and leakage of the river channel are

平原区地下水资源量为 154.6 亿立方米，山丘区与平原区之间的重复计算量为 41.9 亿立方米。黄河流域平原区 1980—2000 年平均地下水可开采量为 119.4 亿立方米，主要分布于上游兰州至河口镇区间和中游龙门至三门峡区间。

3. 地表水天然水化学

黄河流域的地表水大多为重碳酸盐类，矿化度在地区分布上差异较大，低矿化度、中矿化度、较高矿化度和高矿化度水的分布面积，分别占流域总面积的 10.4%、41.9%、27.4% 和 20.3%，其中低矿化度区域主要为黄河源区、秦岭北麓支流，高矿化度区域主要为兰州以下的清水河、苦水河等支流，中矿化度区域为干流兰州以下河段。流域内软水、适度硬水、硬水和极硬水的分布面积，分别占流域总面积的 6.3%、62.9%、14.9% 和 15.9%，总硬度地区分布规律与矿化度基本相同。

依河而生，因河而兴，黄河一直是中华民族的宝藏河流，她无私地敞开胸怀，供人们汲取，让人们在她的滋润下代代昌隆。

名称：《水保协奏曲》　　　　　　　　　　　　作者：党恬敏
Synergy of Water and Soil Protection　　　　Photographer: Dang Tianmin

serious. The drainage area accounts for 20.6% of the whole river, and the annual runoff accounts for only 0.3%.

2. Groundwater Resources

From 1980 to 2000, the annual average groundwater resources in the Yellow River Basin (salinity less than or equal to 2g/L) were 37.60 billion cubic meters, of which groundwater resources were 26.33 billion cubic meters in hilly areas, 15.46 billion cubic meters in plain areas. The repeated amount counted between the area and the plain area is 4.19 billion cubic meters. From 1980 to 2000, the average exploitable groundwater volume in the plain area of the Yellow River Basin was 11.94 billion cubic meters, mainly distributed in the upper reaches between Lanzhou and Hekou Town and the middle reaches between Longmen and Sanmenxia.

3. Natural Water Chemistry of Surface Water

Most of the surface water in the Yellow River Basin is rich in bicarbonate, and the salinity varies greatly in regional distribution. The distribution areas of water with low salinity, medium salinity, relatively high salinity account for 10.4%, 41.9%, 27.4% and 20.3% of the total area of the basin respectively. The low salinity areas are mainly the source area of the Yellow River and the tributaries at the northern foot of the Qinling Mountains, and the high salinity areas are mainly the tributaries in the south of Lanzhou like Qingshui River and Kushui River. The medium salinity area is the main stream in the south of Lanzhou. The distribution areas of soft water, moderate hard water, hard water and extremely hard water in the basin account for 6.3%, 62.9%, 14.9% and 15.9% of the total area of the basin respectively. The regional distribution law of total hardness is basically the same as that of mineralization.

Surviving and thriving along the Yellow River, the Chinese nation views it as the treasure since the Yellow River has offered so much, with which the nation will prosper for generations.

六、生态环境

黄河流域具有较丰富的生态环境类型,沿河形成了各具特色的生物群落。黄河作为连结河源、上中下游及河口等湿地生态单元的"廊道",是维持河流水生生物和洄游鱼类栖息、繁殖的重要基础水系。同时由于特殊的地理环境,黄河流域也是中国生态脆弱区分布面积最大、脆弱生态类型最多、生态脆弱性表现最明显的流域之一。

黄河源区湖泊和沼泽众多,孕育了多种典型高寒生态系统,其中湿地是源区最重要的生态系统,面积约占源区总面积的8.4%,是生物多样性最为集中的区域,且具有较强的水源涵养能力;黄河上游河道外湖泊湿地多属人工和半人工湿地,依靠农灌退水或引黄河水补给水量,湿地对黄河依赖程度较高;中游湿地主要分布在小北干流、三门峡库区等河段;黄河下游受多沙特点的影响,河道淤积摆动变化大,形成了沿河

名称:《生机焕发》　　作者:张延丽

Picture: Vigorousness　　Photographer: Zhang Yanli

VI. Ecology

The Yellow River Basin is rich in ecological environment types and has formed distinctive biomes along the river. As a "corridor" linking the source of the river, the upper, middle and lower reaches of the river and the estuary and other wetland ecological units, the Yellow River is an important basic water system to maintain the river aquatic life and migratory fish habitat and breeding. At the same time, due to the special geographical environment, the Yellow River Basin is also one of the basins with the largest ecologically fragile areas, the most fragile ecological types and the most obvious ecological vulnerability in China.

There are many lakes and marshes in the source area of the Yellow River, which nurture many kinds of typical alpine ecosystems, among which wetlands are the most important ecosystems in the source area with concentrated area of biodiversity, and strong water-holding capacity, accounting for about 8.4% of the total area of the source area. The lakes and wetlands outside the river channel in the upper reaches of the Yellow River are mostly artificial and semi-artificial wetlands, relying on agricultural irrigation receding water or drawing the Yellow River water to recharge water and wetlands depend a lot on the Yellow River. The wetlands in the middle reaches of the Yellow River are mainly located in the Xiaobei main stream, Sanmenxia reservoir area and other river sections; Affected by the large amount of sand, the river siltation oscillation changes greatly in the lower reaches of the Yellow River, forming the washlands along the river in a strip distribution; the Yellow River estuary is in the ecological intersection of land and sea, forming wetlands with abundant natural resources, high biodiversity, which also make up the most extensive and complete native wetland ecosystem in China's warm temperate zone as well as an important "transit point" and wintering, roosting and breeding site for birds migrating from the northeast Asian interior and the western Pacific Ocean.

According to the survey in the 1980s, there are 191 species (subspecies) of fish in the Yellow River Basin, of which 125 species are in the main stream, including 6 species of fish which are either endangered or under national protection. In the upper stream of the Yellow River, especially in the source area, there are plateau

呈带状分布的河漫滩湿地；黄河河口处于海陆生态交错区，湿地自然资源丰富，生物多样性较高，是中国暖温带最广阔、最完整的原生湿地生态系统，也是亚洲东北内陆和环西太平洋鸟类迁徙的重要"中转站"及越冬、栖息和繁殖地。

据 20 世纪 80 年代调查，黄河流域有鱼类 191 种（亚种），干流鱼类有 125 种，其中国家保护鱼类、濒危鱼类 6 种。黄河上游特别是源区分布有拟鲶高原鳅、花斑裸鲤等高原冷水鱼，是黄河特有的土著性鱼类；中下游鱼类以鲤科鱼类为主，多为广布种；下游河口区域鱼类数量及总量相对较多，洄游性鱼类占较高比例，代表性鱼类主要有刀鲚、鲻鱼等。

生态物种的多样化，既有利于中国自然环境的循环协调，也有利于流域社会的安定团结发展。黄河向来都是那样的无私广纳，她有着呵护万物生长的广阔胸襟，也孕育着同样拥有黄河气度的炎黄子民。我们携手砥砺前行，黄河一定会更好。

cold water fish such as catfish, plateau loach and spotted naked carp, which are unique indigenous fish in the Yellow River. The fish in the middle and lower reaches are mainly Cyprinidae, most of which are widely distributed species; The number and total amount of fish in the downstream estuary area are relatively large, and migratory fish account for a high proportion. The representative fish are Coilia nasus, mullet and so on.

The diversification of ecological species is not only conducive to the circular coordination of China's natural environment, but also conducive to the stable and unified development of river basin society. The Yellow River has always been so selfless and inclusive. It has a broad mind to care for the growth of all things, and it also breeds the Yan Huang people who also inherit the bearing of the Yellow River. We will forge ahead hand in hand to create a better Yellow River.

第二章

河南境内典型黄河枢纽工程

Chapter 2

Typical Yellow River Hydro Projects in Henan

黄河是中华文明的摇篮,但纵观历史长河,黄河洪灾泛滥频繁一直是困扰周边流域国计民生的重大难题。自新中国成立以来,黄河的治理开发取得了巨大成就,从龙羊峡到小浪底,干流河道上已建成和即将建成的大中型水电站、水利枢纽共计十四座,形成了中国目前最大的梯级水电站群。国家邮政局2002年6月8日发行《黄河水利水电工程》特种邮票1套4枚,小型张1枚,对黄河治理开发大业留下了生动记录。

The Yellow River is the cradle of Chinese civilization. However, throughout the long history of China, the frequent flooding of the Yellow River has always been a major problem that hindered the development of the national economy and brought sufferings to the livelihood of the public in the surrounding basins. Since the founding of the People's Republic of China, great achievements have been made in the governance and development of the Yellow River. From Longyangxia Reservoir to Xiaolangdi Reservoir, there are a total of 14 large and medium-sized hydropower stations and water conservancy hubs that have been built or will be built on the main stream, forming the largest cascade hydropower station group in China. On June 8, 2002, the State Post Bureau issued a set of four special stamps and one souvenir sheet of Yellow River Water Conservancy and Hydropower Project, which made a vivid record of the great cause of the governance and development of the Yellow River.

The flood control and disaster reduction work of the Yellow River, as well as the development and utilization of its hydropower resources, has promoted the vigorous development of the economy and society in the basin, making the ancient Yellow River glow with youthful vigor and truly become a source of happiness for the benefit of the people. Located on the main stream of the Yellow River in the northern part of Luoyang City, Henan Province, Xiaolangdi Water Conservancy Project is a super-large water conservancy project focusing on flood control, reduction of the menace of ice run and silt reduction, as well as comprehensive utilization of water supply, irrigation and power generation. It is also the exit of the last section of the canyon in the middle reaches of the Yellow River, and is a key part of controlling the water and sediment in the lower reaches of the Yellow River. The project has the characteristics of complex geological conditions, grand construction scale and high construction difficulty, and is known as a "world-class challenging project". Its construction fully proves the ability and wisdom of the contemporary Chinese people in the governance of the Yellow River. In the following paragraph, there will be a brief introduction to the typical water conservancy and hydropower projects of the Yellow River in Henan.

　　黄河的防洪减灾和水电资源的开发利用，促进了流域内经济社会的蓬勃发展，使古老的黄河焕发了青春活力，真真正正成为为民造福的幸福之源。小浪底水利枢纽位于河南省洛阳市北部的黄河干流上，是一座以防洪、防凌、减淤为主，兼顾供水、灌溉、发电的综合利用的特大型水利枢纽。它是黄河中游最后一段峡谷的出口，处于控制黄河下游水沙的关键部位，地质条件复杂，工程建设规模宏伟，施工难度大，被称为"世界级挑战性工程"。它的建成充分体现了当代中国人治理黄河的能力和智慧。下面就针对河南境内典型的黄河水利水电工程做一简要介绍。

一、小浪底水利枢纽

　　小浪底水利枢纽位于河南省洛阳市以北40千米的黄河干流上，南岸属孟津县，北岸属济源市，上距三门峡水利枢纽130千米，下距焦枝铁路桥8千米，距京广铁路郑州黄河铁桥115千米。坝址以上流域面积

Ⅰ. Xiaolangdi Water Conservancy Project

Xiaolangdi Water Conservancy Project is located on the main stream of the Yellow River, 40 kilometers north of Luoyang City, Henan Province. Its south bank is in Mengjin County, and its north bank is in Jiyuan City. It is 130 kilometers away from Sanmenxia Water Conservancy Project above, 8 kilometers away from Jiaozhi Railway Bridge at the bottom, and 115 kilometers away from Zhengzhou Yellow River Iron Bridge on Beijing-Guangzhou Railway. The basin area above the dam site reaches 694,155 square kilometers.

Its pivotal buildings include dams, flood discharging tunnels, sand discharging tunnels, power generation and water diversion tunnels, power plant workshops, power plant tailrace tunnels, flood spillways and irrigation and diversion tunnels. The dams are divided into the main dam and the auxiliary dam. The main dam is located in the river bed and is a rockfill dam with a loam core-wall. The dam crest is 1,317.34 meters long, 15 meters wide, 281 meters high, and the maximum dam height is 154 meters. The auxiliary dam is located at the bealock on the left bank, and is a loam core-wall rockfill dam. The dam crest is 170 meters long and the dam crest elevation is 280 meters. The flood discharging tunnel is located in the mountain on the left bank, and its entrance is in the wind and rain ditch. The flood discharging tunnel is divided into the orifice plate flood discharging tunnel and the open flow flood discharging tunnel.

Xiaolangdi Water Conservancy Project focuses on flood control, reduction of the menace of ice run and silt reduction, as well as comprehensive utilization of water supply, irrigation and power generation. The normal water storage level of the project is 275 meters, the dead water level is 230 meters, the design flood level is 274 meters, and the check flood level is 275 meters. Its total storage capacity is 12.65 billion cubic meters(the normal water level is below 275 meters), of which the flood control storage capacity is 4.05 billion cubic meters, the adjustment storage capacity is 5.1 billion cubic meters, and the dead storage capacity is 7.55 billion cubic meters.

Xiaolangdi Water Conservancy Project is the only controlled project below Sanmenxia, the main stream of the Yellow River, that has a large storage capacity. It can control the flood of the Yellow River, and its sediment storage capacity can

694155平方千米。

枢纽建筑物包括大坝、泄洪洞、排沙洞、发电引水隧洞、电站厂房、电站尾水洞、溢洪道和灌溉引水洞。大坝分主坝和副坝。主坝位于河床中，为壤土斜心墙堆石坝，坝顶长1317.34米，宽15米，坝顶高程281米，最大坝高154米。副坝位于左岸分水岭垭口处，为壤土心墙堆石坝，坝顶长170米，坝顶高程280米。泄洪洞位于左岸山体内，进口位于风雨沟，分孔板泄洪洞和明流泄洪洞。

小浪底水利枢纽的任务以防洪、防凌、减淤为主，兼顾供水、灌溉和发电。枢纽正常蓄水位高程275米，死水位230米，设计洪水位274米，校核洪水位275米；总库容126.5亿立方米（正常蓄水位高程275米以下），其中防洪库容40.5亿立方米，调节库容51亿立方米，死库容75.5亿立方米。

小浪底水利枢纽是黄河干流三门峡以下唯一能够取得较大库容的控制性工程，既可较好地控制黄河洪水，又可利用其淤沙库容拦截泥沙，进行调水调沙运用，以减缓下游河床的淤积抬高。1991年4月，七届全国人大四次会议批准小浪底工程在"八五"期间动工兴建。1991年9月1日前期准备工程开工。主体工程于1994年9月12日开工。1997年10月28日，小浪底工程顺利实现大河截流。历时6年，2000年11月30日，大坝主体全部完工。2000年1月9日，首台机组投产。2001年12月31日，工程全部竣工，总工期11年。2002年至2008年，小浪底工程先后通过了安全技术鉴定、水土保持、工程档案、消防设施、环境保护、劳动安全卫生等专项验收。2008年12月，小浪底工程通过竣工技术预验收。2009年4月7日，小浪底工程顺利通过由国家发展和改革委员会、水利部共同主持的竣工验收，被世界银行誉为该行与发展中国家合作项目的典范。

be used to block sediment, so as to adjust water and sediment, thus slowing down the sediment accumulation of the downstream riverbed. In April 1991, the Fourth Session of the Seventh National People's Congress approved the construction of Xiaolangdi Project during the "Eighth Five-Year Plan" period. On September 1, 1991, the preparatory works started, and its main project started on September 12, 1994. On October 28, 1997, Xiaolangdi Project successfully realized the closure of the river. On November 30, 2000, the main body of the dam was completed after six years. On January 9, 2000, the first unit was put into operation. On December 31, 2001, the project was completed, with a total construction period of 11 years. From 2002 to 2008, Xiaolangdi Project passed the special acceptance checks of safety technical appraisal, the soil and water conservation, engineering archives, fire protection facilities, environmental protection, labor safety and health, etc. In December 2008, Xiaolangdi Project passed the construction technology pre-acceptance check. On April 7, 2009, Xiaolangdi Project successfully passed the completion acceptance check jointly presided by the National Development and Reform Commission and the Ministry of Water Resources, and is hailed by the World Bank as a model of the cooperation projects of the bank with developing countries.

小浪底水利枢纽
Xiaolangdi Water Conservancy Project

二、三门峡水利枢纽

三门峡水利枢纽位于黄河中游下段干流上，两岸连接豫、晋两省，在河南省三门峡市东北约 17 千米处。坝址以上流域面积 68.8 万平方千米，占全流域面积的 91.5%。

枢纽建筑物包括混凝土重力坝、斜丁坝、表孔、底孔、泄洪排沙洞、泄流排水钢管、电站厂房。混凝土重力坝坝顶全长 713.20 米，坝顶高程 353 米，最大坝高 106 米。正常高水位 350 米高程时相应总库容 354 亿立方米。电站厂房位于电站坝段下游，设计装机 116 万千瓦，改建后（至 1994 年底）装机为 32.5 万千瓦，库区实际移民 40.37 万人，淹没耕地 90 万亩。工程原建和两期改建共完成土石方 1871 万立方米，混凝土 212 万立方米，共投资 94357.3 万元。

枢纽的任务是防洪、防凌、灌溉、发电、供水。于 1957 年 4 月动工兴建，1960 年 9 月基本建成投入使用。枢纽主体工程由苏联电站部水力发电设计院列宁格勒分院设计，三门峡工程局施工。三门峡水利枢纽是根据"除害兴利，蓄水拦沙"治黄方针兴建的第一座高坝大库工程，是治理和开发黄河的一次重大实践。

枢纽按正常高水位 360 米高程设计，为减少淹没，国务院决定初期按正常高水位 350 米高程施工，运用水位不超过 340 米高程，控制在 333 米高程以下。1960 年按"蓄水拦沙"运用后库区淤积严重，"黄河技经报告"所预计的三门峡以上减少泥沙的效果短期内难以达到，引发了一场以三门峡水利枢纽工程为中心的治黄方针大争论。在工程建设和运用过程中，对工程开发任务和运用方式，存在着不同的主张。为了减缓库区淤积，先后对工程进行两次改建，水库运用方式也进行了两次改变，1973 年以来按"蓄清排浑"运用，库区淤积大为减缓。工程建成后，虽未达到原设计要求的效益，但仍具有防洪、防凌、灌溉、发电、供水

II. Sanmenxia Water Conservancy Project

Sanmenxia Water Conservancy Project is located on the main stream of the lower section of the middle reaches of the Yellow River. Its two sides connect Henan and Shanxi provinces, and its address is about 17 kilometers northeast of Sanmenxia City, Henan Province. The area of the watershed above the dam site is 688,000 square kilometers, accounting for 91.5% of the total watershed area.

The buildings of the project include: concrete gravity dam, inclined spur dam, surface hole, bottom hole, flood discharging and sand discharging holes, discharging and drainage steel pipe, power station workshop, etc. The total length of the crest of the concrete gravity dam is 713.20 meters, the elevation of the dam crest is 353 meters, and the maximum dam height is 106 meters. When its normal high water level is 350 meters above sea level, the corresponding total storage capacity is 35.4 billion cubic meters. The powerhouse of the power station is located downstream of the dam section of the power station. The designed installed power is 1.16 million kilowatts, and the installed power after the reconstruction (by the end of 1994) is 325,000 kilowatts. The actual resettlement in the reservoir area was 403,700 people, and the construction of the project submerged 900,000 *mu* of arable land. A total of 18.71 million cubic meters of earthwork and 2.12 million cubic meters of concrete have been completed for the original construction and the two-phase reconstruction of the project, with a total investment of 943.573 million yuan.

The tasks of the project include flood control, reduction of the menace of ice run, irrigation, power generation and water supply. The project started construction in April 1957 and was basically completed and put into use in September 1960. The main engineering of the project was designed by the Leningrad Branch of the Hydropower Design Institute of the Soviet Power Station Ministry, and constructed by the Sanmenxia Engineering Bureau. Sanmenxia Water Conservancy Project is not only the first high-dam reservoir project built according to the policy of "eliminating dangers and prospering profits, accumulating water and blocking sand", but also a major practice in the governance and development of the Yellow River.

The project is designed according to the normal high water level of 360

等效益。中共中央和国务院十分重视三门峡工程的建设，曾把其列为苏联援建的156项工程中唯一的一项水利工程。周恩来总理曾三次深入工程现场研究解决工程建设和运用中的问题，中央其他领导人也曾多次深入现场指导。由于对泥沙淤积严重性认识不足和对水土保持及拦泥工程减沙效果估计过高，库区严重淤积，被迫对工程进行两次改建，枢纽运用方式经历了"蓄水拦沙"和"滞洪排沙"运用阶段，后改为"蓄清排浑"运用，发挥了枢纽调水调沙的重大作用。三门峡水利枢纽工程的实践，使人们对黄河水沙规律特殊性的认识得到了提高，为多沙河流的开发治理提供了宝贵经验。

三门峡水利枢纽

Sanmenxia Water Conservancy Project

meters. In order to reduce inundation, the State Council decided to carry out construction according to the normal high water level of 350 meters in the initial stage, and resettle based on the water level of not exceeding 340 meters, the control of below 333 meters. In 1960, after the application of "accumulating water and blocking sand", the reservoir area was seriously silted up. As a result, the effect of reducing sediment above Sanmenxia, as predicted by the Yellow River Technical Economic Report, can hardly be realized in the short term, thus triggering a major debate on the Yellow River governance policy centered on the Sanmenxia Water Conservancy Project. Experts have different opinions on the engineering development tasks and application methods in the process of engineering construction and application. In order to slow down the siltation in the reservoir area, the project has been reconstructed twice, and the way of using the reservoir has also been changed twice. Since 1973, the application of "storing clean water and draining muddy water" has greatly slowed down the sedimentation in the reservoir area. After the project was completed, although we found that it did not achieve the benefits of the original design, it still had benefits of flood control, reduction of the menace of ice run, irrigation, power generation and water supply. The Central Committee of the CPC and the State Council attached great importance to the construction of the Sanmenxia Project, and once listed it as the only water conservancy project among the 156 projects supported by the Soviet Union. Premier Zhou Enlai went to the project site three times to study and help solve problems in project construction and application, and other leaders of the central government have also gone into the field many times to provide guidance. The reservoir area was seriously silted up, and the project was forced to be rebuilt twice, due to the underestimation of the seriousness of sediment deposition and the overestimation of soil and water conservation as well as the sediment reduction effect of the silt retaining project. The application method of the project was changed from "accumulating water and blocking sand" and "flood retention and sediment discharge" to "storing clean water and draining muddy water", thus playing a major role in water and sediment regulation of the project. The practice of the Sanmenxia Water Conservancy Project has improved the public understanding of the particularity of the water and sediment regulations of the Yellow River, while the construction of this project has provided valuable experience for the development and governance of sandy rivers.

三、故县水库

故县水库位于黄河支流洛河中游洛宁县境故县镇,东距洛阳市165千米,控制流域面积5370平方千米,占洛河流域面积(不含支流伊河面积)的41.8%。故县水库工程于1958年开工兴建,1992年基本建成,经历了"三下四上"的漫长过程。1958年10月首次兴工"上马",1960年停建;1970年春第一次复工,当年底停工缓建;1973年第二次复工,1975年底又停工缓建;1978年初第三次复工。工程设计方案和施工队伍几经变动,因为工程的相关规模、效益、工期、协作、投资等计划一直未能敲定,直至1992年才基本竣工。1993年10月,水利部对故县水库工程进行竣工初步验收。1994年1月20日国家验收委员会组织竣工验收。

故县水库
Guxian Reservoir

III. Guxian Reservoir

Guxian Reservoir is located in Guxian Town, Luoning County, which is along the middle reaches of Luohe River, a tributary of the Yellow River, 165 kilometers east of Luoyang City. The basin area under its control is 5,370 square kilometers, accounting for 41.8% of the area of the Luo River basin (excluding the area of the tributary Yihe River). The Guxian Reservoir Project started in 1958 and was basically completed in 1992. Its construction process has gone through a long process of "three stops and four starts". It was first constructed in October 1958 and stopped in 1960. In the spring of 1970, it resumed work for the first time, but stopped construction at the end of that year. In 1973, it resumed work for the second time, and at the end of 1975, the construction was suspended again. In early 1978, the project resumed work for the third time. The design scheme and construction team of the project have undergone several changes. Because the relevant scale, benefit, construction period, collaboration, investment and other plans of the project have not been finalized, the project was not basically completed until 1992. In October 1993, the Ministry of Water Resources carried out preliminary acceptance check of the Guxian Reservoir Project. On January 20, 1994, the National Acceptance Committee organized the final acceptance check.

Guxian Reservoir Project is an important project in the flood control system in the middle and lower reaches of the Yellow River. The task of the reservoir is mainly to prevent floods, and it also has functions such as irrigation, power generation, and water supply. The project has the advantages of reasonable design and excellent construction quality. Since it was put into operation, the reservoir has successfully brought into play the benefits of flood control, irrigation, power generation, and fish farming. The building of the reservoir consists of the barrage, the powerhouse and the drainage channels in the attached dam. Its barrage is a concrete solid gravity dam with a maximum dam height of 125 meters and a total storage capacity of 1.175 billion cubic meters. The dam crest elevation is 553 meters, the dam crest is 9 meters wide and 315 meters long. The dam consists of

故县水库工程是黄河中下游防洪体系中的一项重要工程，水库任务主要是以防洪为主，兼有灌溉、发电、供水等。工程设计合理，施工质量优良，投入运行以来，发挥了防洪、灌溉、发电、养鱼等效益。水库建筑物由拦河坝、电站厂房及附设坝体内的泄水孔道组成。拦河坝为混凝土实体重力坝，最大坝高 125 米，总库容 11.75 亿立方米，坝顶高程 553 米，坝顶宽 9 米，坝顶长 315 米，由挡水坝段、电站坝段、底孔坝段、溢流坝段及中孔坝段组成，共 21 个坝段，坝段一般长 16.5 米，最长 19 米，最短 13 米。

a retaining dam section, a power station dam section, a bottom hole dam section, an overflow dam section and a middle hole dam section, with a total of 21 dam sections. The dam section is generally 16.5 meters long, with a maximum of 19 meters and a minimum of 13 meters.

四、陆浑水库

陆浑水库位于河南省洛阳市嵩县田湖镇陆浑村附近，黄河二级支流伊河上，距洛阳市 67 千米，控制流域面积 3492 平方千米，占伊河流域面积的 57.9%。坝址处多年平均年径流量 10.25 亿立方米（1951—1968 年），多年平均流量 32.5 立方米每秒，多年平均年输沙量约 300 万吨，平均含沙量 3.2 千克每立方米，泥沙 90% 以上集中在汛期（7—10 月），非汛期河水清澈见底。千年一遇洪峰流量 12400 立方米每秒，万年一遇洪峰流量 17100 立方米每秒，保坝洪水（万年一遇洪峰加 20%）洪峰流量 20520 立方米每秒。坝址位于嵩县盆地出口峡谷地段，峡谷长 500 米，峡谷上游盆地宽 3000—4000 米，坝址处河床宽 320 米。

陆浑水库
Luhun Reservoir

IV. Luhun Reservoir

Luhun Reservoir is located near Luhun Village, Tianhu Town, Song County, Luoyang City, Henan Province. It is located on the Yihe River, a secondary tributary of the Yellow River, 67 kilometers away from Luoyang City. The area of its control basin is 3,492 square kilometers, accounting for 57.9% of the area of the Yihe River Basin. The multi-year average annual runoff at the dam site was 1.025 billion cubic meters (1951-1968), the multi-year average flow rate is 32.5m^3/s, the multi-year average annual sediment transport is about 3 million tons, and the average sediment content is 3.2kg/m^3. More than 90% of the sediment is concentrated in the flood season from July to October. During the non-flood season, the river water is crystal clear. The flow of the once-in-a-thousand-year flood peak can reach 12,400m^3/s, the flow of the once-in-ten-thousand-year flood peak can reach 17,100m^3/s, and the peak flow of the dam protection flood (the once-in-a-million-year flood peak plus 20%) can reach 20,520m^3/s. The dam site is located in the canyon section at the exit of the Song County Basin. The canyon is 500 meters long, the basin upstream of the canyon is 3,000 to 4,000 meters wide, and the riverbed at the dam site is 320 meters wide.

The main buildings of the reservoir include barrage(clay inclined wall sand shell dam), water delivery tunnels, flood discharging tunnels, irrigation and power generation tunnels, spillways and power stations (There are three electrical machines in the water delivery tunnel power station, each of which has the capacity of 1,250 kilowatts. And there are three electrical machines in the irrigation tunnel power station, one with 3,000 kilowatts, one with 3,200 kilowatts, and the other with 500 kilowatts). The total installed power of the power station is 10,450 kilowatts. The flood level elevations of the 1000-year flood design and the 10,000-year flood check of the reservoir are respectively 327.5 meters (the Yellow Sea elevation system) and 331.8 meters. The elevation of the normal high water level is 319.5 meters, and the elevation of the dam crest is 333 meters. The main tasks of the reservoir are flood control, irrigation, power generation and water supply. The height of the dam is 55 meters, and its total

水库主要建筑物包括拦河坝（黏土斜墙砂壳坝）、输水洞、泄洪洞、灌溉发电洞、溢洪道和电站（输水洞电站装机 3 台，单机容量 1250 千瓦；灌溉洞电站装机 3 台，1 台 3000 千瓦，1 台 3200 千瓦，1 台 500 千瓦）。电站总装机 1.045 万千瓦。水库千年一遇洪水设计，万年一遇洪水校核，洪水位高程分别为 327.5 米（黄海高程系）和 331.8 米，正常高水位高程 319.5 米，坝顶高程 333 米。水库的主要任务是防洪、灌溉发电和供水。坝高 55 米，总库容 13.2 亿立方米。工程于 1959 年 12 月开始兴建，1965 年 8 月底建成。灌溉发电洞 1972 年 2 月开始增建，1974 年 7 月建成。1976 年开始水库保坝加固工程施工，1988 年一期加固工程完成。共完成土石方 705.61 万立方米，混凝土 14.86 万立方米。工程共计投资 1.68 亿元。

storage capacity is 1.32 billion cubic meters. The construction of the reservoir began in December 1959 and was completed by the end of August 1965. The irrigation and power generation cave expanded its construction in February 1972 and completed in July 1974. In 1976, the construction of the reinforcement of the reservoir dam started, and in 1988 the first phase of the reinforcement was completed. The whole project used a total of 7.0561 million cubic meters of earth and stone, and 148,600 cubic meters of concrete, with a total investment of 168 million yuan.

五、西霞院反调节水库

西霞院反调节水库是黄河小浪底水利枢纽的配套工程,位于小浪底坝址下游 16 千米处的黄河干流上,下距郑州市 116 千米。

西霞院反调节水库
Xixiayuan Counter-Regulation Reservoir

西霞院反调节水库主要建筑物有土石坝、泄洪闸、排沙闸、河床式电站厂房、王庄引水闸、坝后灌溉引水闸及电站安装间下排沙洞等,坝轴线总长 3122 米,其中混凝土坝段(泄洪、发电、引水)长 513 米。泄水、发电建筑物集中布置在右岸滩地,共设置 21 孔泄洪闸,排沙建筑物包括电站厂房左侧的排沙洞、右侧的排沙闸和机组之间的排沙底孔,王庄引水闸位于泄洪闸右侧,灌溉引水闸位于电站下游左侧岸边。左右岸滩地和河槽段为土工膜斜墙砂砾石坝,最大坝高 20.2 米,坝顶宽 8.0 米,坝顶高程 138.2 米,上游边坡坡度 1∶2.75,下游边坡坡度 1∶2.25。其中左岸(含河槽段)坝长 1725.5 米,右岸坝长 883.5 米,砂砾石坝总

V. Xixiayuan Counter-Regulation Reservoir

Xixiayuan Counter-Regulation Reservoir is a supporting project of Xiaolangdi Water Control Project on the Yellow River. It is located on the main stream of the Yellow River, which is 16 kilometers downstream of the Xiaolangdi dam site, and it is 116 kilometers away from Zhengzhou.

The main buildings of Xixiayuan Counter-Regulation Reservoir include the earth-rock dam, flood discharging gate, sand discharging gate, riverbed-type power plant, Wangzhuang diversion gate, irrigation diversion gate behind the dam and the sand drainage hole under the power station installation room, etc. The total length of the axis of the dam is 3,122 meters, of which the length of the concrete dam section (flood release, power generation, water diversion) is 513 meters. The buildings for water discharge and power generation are concentrated on the beach on the right bank, and a total of 21 flood discharging gates are set in this area. The buildings for sand discharging include the sand discharging hole on the left side of the power plant, the sand discharging gate on the right and the bottom hole for sand discharging between the units. Wangzhuang diversion gate is located on the right side of the flood gate. The irrigation diversion gate is located on the left bank downstream of the power station. The beach and river channel sections on the left and right banks are gravel stone dams with geomembrane inclined walls. The maximum height of the dam is 20.2 meters, the width of the dam crest is 8.0 meters, and the elevation of the dam crest is 138.2 meters. The upstream slope is 1 : 2.75, and the downstream slope is 1 : 2.25. The length of the dam on the left bank (including the channel section) is 1,725.5 meters, the length of the dam on the right bank is 883.5 meters, and the total length of the gravel dam is 2,609 meters. The hydropower station adopts a riverbed-type powerhouse with a maximum height of 51.5 meters. The hydropower station is equipped with four axial-flow rotary-paddle hydro-generator units with a single unit capacity of 35 megawatts. The total installed capacity is 140 megawatts, and the multi-year average power generation is 583 million kilowatts per hour. The anti-seepage treatment of the dam foundation adopts concrete anti-seepage wall, and the project scale belongs to the second largest group according to the Chinese

长 2609 米。水电站为河床式厂房，最大高度为 51.5 米，设有 4 台单机容量为 35 兆瓦的轴流转浆式水轮发电机组，总装机容量 140 兆瓦，多年平均发电量 5.83 亿千瓦·时。坝基防渗采用混凝土防渗墙。工程规模为大（2）型。水库总库容 1.62 亿立方米，正常蓄水位 134 米，汛期限制水位 131 米。

西霞院工程的开发任务是以反调节为主，结合发电，兼顾灌溉、供水等综合利用。工程概算总投资 21.97 亿元，其中由小浪底水利枢纽建设管理局筹资 5 亿元，其余部分由国家投资。前期准备工程从 2003 年元月开工，工期 1 年；主体工程于 2004 年元月开工，工期 4.5 年；2007 年 6 月 18 日，首台机组并网发电；2008 年 1 月 4 台机组全部并网发电。截至 2010 年 12 月 31 日，西霞院水电站已连续安全运行 1293 天，累计发电量 14.84 亿千瓦·时。工程在反调节、发电、供水等方面取得了显著效益。2011 年 3 月 2 日，西霞院工程顺利通过国家竣工验收。

standard. The total storage capacity of the reservoir is 162 million cubic meters, the normal water level is 134 meters, and the limited water level during the flood season is 131 meters.

The development task of Xixiayuan Counter-Regulation Reservoir is mainly focused on counter-regulation, and it combines the comprehensive utilization of irrigation, water supply, etc. The estimated total investment of the project is 2.197 billion yuan, of which 500 million yuan was raised by Xiaolangdi Construction Management Bureau, and the rest was invested by the state. The preparatory works in the early stage started in January 2003, with a construction period of one year. The main project started in January 2004 with a construction period of 4.5 years. On June 18, 2007, the first unit was connected to the grid for power generation. In January 2008, all four units were connected to the grid to generate electricity. As of December 31, 2010, Xixiayuan Counter-Regulation Reservoir has been running safely for 1,293 consecutive days, with a cumulative power generation of 1.484 billion kilowatts per hour. The project has achieved remarkable benefits in anti-regulation, power generation and water supply. On March 2, 2011, Xixiayuan project successfully passed the acceptance assessment of China.

六、河口村水库

沁河河口村水库工程位于沁河干流最后峡谷段出口五龙口以上约9千米处,控制流域面积9223平方千米,占沁河流域面积的68.2%。水库距河南省济源市约20千米,属济源市克井镇。河口村水库是一座以防洪、供水为主,兼顾灌溉、发电、改善河道基流等综合利用的大型水利枢纽,工程位于黄河一级支流沁河最后一段峡谷出口处,是黄河下游防洪工程体系的主要组成部分,是国家对中部地区建设大型水库的最高补助投资项目。

河口村水库
Hekou Village Reservoir

早在1959年黄河水利委员会勘测规划设计研究院即对河口村水库进行了现场勘探,1968年9月,河南省在沁河下游规划报告中要求兴建河口村水库。2011年3月2日,河南省沁河河口村水库工程可行性研究报告获国家发改委批复。经过近半个世纪的努力,在三门峡至花园口区间的黄河干支流上已建成三门峡水利枢纽,在黄河支流上已建成故县

Ⅵ. Hekou Village Reservoir

Qinhe Hekou Village Reservoir Project is located about 9 kilometers above Wulongkou, the exit of the last canyon section of the mainstream of Qinhe River. The control basin area of the project is 9,223 square kilometers, accounting for 68.2% of the Qinhe basin area. The reservoir is about 20 kilometers away from Jiyuan City, Henan Province, and it belongs to Kejing Town, Jiyuan City. Hekou Village Reservoir is a large-scale water conservancy project focusing on flood control and water supply, as well as comprehensive utilization of irrigation, power generation, and improvement of river base flow. The project is located at the exit of the last canyon of the Qinhe River, a first-class tributary of the Yellow River. It is not only the main component of the flood control engineering system in the lower reaches of the Yellow River, but also the highest subsidy investment project of China for the construction of large reservoirs in the central region.

As early as 1959, the Yellow River Survey, Planning and Design Co., Ltd. conducted the on-site exploration of the Hekou Village Reservoir. In September 1968, Henan Province requested the construction of Hekou Village Reservoir in the Planning Report on the Lower Reaches of Qinhe River. On March 2, 2011, the feasibility study report of the Qinhe Hekou Village Reservoir Project in Henan Province was approved by the National Development and Reform Commission. After the hard work of nearly half a century, Sanmenxia Water Conservancy Project has been built on the main and tributaries of the Yellow River between Sanmenxia and Huayuankou. Guxian and Luhun reservoirs have been built on the tributaries of the Yellow River. The lower reaches of the Yellow River have initially formed a flood control engineering system of "detaining in the upper stream, discharging in the lower stream, and retarding on both shores". The flood control capacity has been greatly improved, but there is still the possibility of serious floods downstream.

With the accumulation of the dead storage capacity of the Xiaolangdi Project, the frequent encounter of floods in the Qinhe River and the floods in the Yellow River is one of the main sources of large floods in the uncontrolled area from Xiaolangdi to Huayuankou. This is the reason for the construction of Hekou

水库、陆浑水库，黄河下游已初步形成"上拦下排、两岸分滞"的防洪工程体系，防洪能力已有很大提高，但下游仍有发生大洪水的可能。

随着小浪底水库死库容的淤积，沁河洪水和黄河洪水经常遭遇，是小浪底至花园口无控制区大洪水的主要来源之一，因此兴建了河口村水库。工程设有大坝、溢洪道、泄洪洞、引水发电洞、电站厂房等建筑物，总库容 3.17 亿立方米，最大坝高 122.5 米。水库建成后，可减轻黄河防洪压力，同时将使南水北调总干渠穿沁工程达到 100 年一遇的防洪标准，也可使沁河防洪标准由当前不足 25 年一遇提高到 100 年一遇。对减轻黄河下游的洪水威胁，减少黄河滩区中常洪水的淹没损失以及缓解沁河下游水资源供需矛盾具有重要的意义。

Village Reservoir. The dams, spillways, flood discharging tunnels, diversion power generation tunnels, power station workshops and other buildings are built for the project, with a total storage capacity of 317 million cubic meters and a maximum dam height of 122.5m. The reservoir can reduce the flood control pressure of the Yellow River after its completion. It will make the main canal of the South-to-North Water Diversion Project meet the one-in-one-hundred-year design flood control standard, and also increase the flood control standard of the Qinhe River from the current one-in-25 years to a one-in-100 years. The completion of this project is of great significance for alleviating the threat of floods in the lower reaches of the Yellow River, reducing the inundation loss of frequent floods in the Yellow River floodplain, and alleviating the contradiction between supply and demand of water resources in the downstream of the Qinhe River.

七、郑州黄河铁路大桥

郑州黄河铁路大桥位于黄河下游河道的上端,原黄河铁桥下游 500 米处,北岸是河南省武陟县老田庵村,南岸为黄河大堤 0+730 处。于 1958 年 5 月开工建设,1960 年 4 月建成通车。如今,有着 60 多年运营史的郑州黄河铁路大桥在中国铁路交通运输网格局中发挥着至关重要的作用。现在的郑州黄河铁路大桥由北岸引桥、主桥、南岸引桥三部分组成,全长 2889.8 米,桥面宽 12.5 米。

该大桥是京广线上的双线铁路桥。原郑州黄河铁路大桥建成于 1905 年 11 月,由清政府交比利时公司承建,是当时卢沟桥至汉口铁路(后改称京汉铁路)工程中的一项关键工程。1906 年 4 月京汉铁路的全线贯通打破了以往仅依赖于水道与驿道的传统交通网络格局,促进了铁路沿线地区的较快发展。

郑州黄河铁路大桥
The Zhengzhou Yellow River Railway Brideg

Ⅶ. The Zhengzhou Yellow River Railway Bridge

The Zhengzhou Yellow River Railway Bridge is located at the upper end of the lower reaches of the Yellow River, 500m downstream of the original Yellow River Iron Bridge. The north bank is Laotian'an Village, Wuzhi County, Henan Province, and the south bank is the Yellow River Embankment 0+730. Construction started in May 1958 and was completed and opened to traffic in April, 1960. Today, the Zhengzhou Yellow River Railway Bridge, with more than 60 years of operation history, plays a vital role in the China Railway Transportation Network. The current Zhengzhou Yellow River Railway Bridge consists of three parts: the north bank approach bridge, the main bridge and the south bank approach bridge, with a total length of 2,889.8m and a bridge deck width of 12.5m.

The bridge is a double-track railway bridge on the Beijing-Guangzhou line. The original Zhengzhou Yellow River Railway Bridge was completed in November, 1905. It was contracted by the Qing government to the Belgian company. It was a key project in the Lugou Bridge-Hankou Railway (later renamed Jinghan Railway) at that time. In April 1906, when the entire Jinghan Railway was completed, it broke the traditional traffic network pattern that only relied on waterways and post roads, and promoted the rapid development of the areas along the railway.

Shortly after the founding of the People's Republic of China, the Ministry of Railways started to prepare for the construction of the Wuhan Yangtze River Bridge in response to the urgent need for the rapid growth of railway traffic. In 1957, the Wuhan Yangtze River Bridge was built, and the Jinghan Railway connected the Yuehan Railway, collectively known as the Beijing-Guangzhou Railway, with a total length of 2,263km.

Since then, the state has made great efforts to speed up the construction of the double line of the Beijing-Guangzhou Railway. In 1960, the current Zhengzhou Yellow River Railway Bridge was built. The second line of the Hankou-Hengyang section and the Hengyang-Guangzhou section was also opened to traffic. In 1988, the double track of the Beijing-Guangzhou Railway

新中国成立后不久，根据铁路运量迅速增长的迫切需要，铁道部即着手筹建武汉长江大桥。1957年武汉长江大桥建成，京汉铁路连通了粤汉铁路，合称京广铁路，全长达到2263千米。

此后，国家着力加快京广铁路复线建设，1960年建成了现在的郑州黄河铁路大桥，汉口至衡阳段、衡阳至广州段第二线工程也先后通车。1988年京广铁路复线全线开通，成为纵贯中国南北的交通大动脉。

纵观河南境内的诸多黄河水利枢纽工程，既有新中国成立后第一座大型水利枢纽，被称为"千里黄河第一坝"的三门峡水利枢纽；也有"黄河的总阀门"——小浪底大坝；更有被称作"中国铁路桥梁之母"的"万里黄河第一桥"——郑州黄河铁路大桥。

它们不仅仅保障着黄河下游两岸人民群众的饮水安全、粮食安全、用电安全，更是对新中国成立后"兴水利，除水害"的真实记录。如今，黄河流域的生态保护和高质量发展更离不开黄河枢纽工程的协同调度，唯有让黄河上的各个水利枢纽工程各司其职，方能保障黄河成为造福人民的幸福河！

was fully opened, and it becomes China's north-to-south traffic artery.

Regarding of the many water conservancy projects on the Yellow River in Henan, there is not only the Sanmenxia Water Conservancy Project, the first large-scale water conservancy project after the founding of the People's Republic of China, known as "the First Dam of the One-thousand-mile Yellow River", but also the Xiaolangdi Dam, known as "the Master Valve of the Yellow River". There is the Zhengzhou Yellow River Railway Bridge, known as the "Mother of China's Railway Bridges" and "the First Bridge of the Ten-thousand-mile Yellow River"...

They not only ensure the safety of drinking water, food, and electricity for the people on both sides of the lower reaches of the Yellow River, but are also a true record of "promoting water conservancy and eliminating water hazards" after the founding of the People's Republic of China. Today, the ecological protection and high-quality development of the Yellow River Basin are more inseparable from the coordinated scheduling of the Yellow River hub project. Only by letting each water conservancy project on the Yellow River perform its own duties can we ensure that the Yellow River becomes a happy river for the benefit of the people!

第三章

黄河流域水利工程对生态保护的意义

Chapter 3

Significance of the Yellow River Basin Water Conservancy Project for Ecological Protection

中国位于亚欧大陆的东南部，西北部深入亚欧大陆腹地，东南部濒临太平洋。因此，中国大部分地区属于海陆交相影响的季风区，只有西北部属于极为干燥的大陆性气候。由于季风气候存在不确定性，因而中国的降水及河川径流年内集中、年际变化大等情况比地球上同纬度的欧洲国家更明显。同时，中国地势的特点是西高东低，呈阶梯状分布，从而导致河流大都是自西向东流注入海洋。在中国大江大河的中下游地区，集中了全国半数以上的人口、三分之一的耕地和70%的工农业产值，是中国经济社会发展的核心所在。然而，这些地区的地面高度有不少是处在江河洪水位以下，洪灾的潜在影响始终威胁着经济建设和人民群众的正常生活。为了满足控制洪水和灌溉兴利的需要，河流的上中游地区是水利工程选址的首选地区。

水利枢纽工程是为满足各项水利工程兴利除害的目标，在河流或渠道的适宜地段修建的不同类型水工建筑物的综合体。水利枢纽常以其形成的水库或主体工程——坝、水电站的名称来命名，如三峡大坝、陆浑水库、故县水库、龙羊峡水电站等；也有直接称水利枢纽的，如小浪底水利枢纽、三门峡水利枢纽。随着这些地区水利工程的不断修建，河流的天然水文环境发生了极大变化，水利枢纽工程在防洪、灌溉、供水和发电等方面发挥重要作用的同时，其建设和运行对生态环境也产生了较大影响。

一、黄河流域环境变迁

黄河流域的环境变迁，是一个漫长的变化过程，可追溯到距今1万年前。

Chapter 3 Significance of the Yellow River Basin Water Conservancy Project for Ecological Protection

China is located in the southeastern part of the Asian and European continent, with the northwestern part deep in the Asian and European hinterland and the southeastern part bordering the Pacific Ocean. Therefore, most of China belongs to the monsoon area where sea and land intersect, and only the northwestern part belongs to the extremely dry continental climate. Because of the uncertainty of monsoon climate, the situation of concentrated precipitation and river runoff within the year and large interannual variation in China is more obvious and serious than that of European countries at the same latitude on earth. At the same time, the topography of China is characterized by high west and low east, with a stepped distribution, which results in most rivers flowing from west to east into the ocean. In the middle and lower reaches of China's major rivers, more than half of the country's population, one-third of its arable land and 70% of its industrial and agricultural output are concentrated, making them the core of China's economic and social development. However, many of the ground heights in these areas are below the flood level of rivers, and the potential impact of flooding always threatens the economic construction and normal life of the people. In order to meet the needs of flood control and irrigation, the upstream and midstream areas of rivers are the preferred areas for siting water conservancy projects.

The hydraulic hub project is a complex of different types of hydraulic buildings constructed in suitable sections of rivers or channels to meet the objectives of each water conservancy project to promote the benefit and eliminate the harm. Hydraulic hubs are often named after the name of the reservoir or main project—dam, hydropower station, such as the Three Gorges Dam, Luhun Reservoir, Guxian Reservoir, Longyangxia Hydropower Station, etc.; some are also directly called hydraulic hubs, such as Xiaolangdi Water Resources Hub, Sanmenxia Water Resources Hub. With the continuous construction of water conservancy projects in these areas, the natural hydrological environment of rivers has changed dramatically. While water conservancy hub projects play an important role in flood control, irrigation, water supply and power generation, their construction and operation also have a greater impact on the ecological environment.

1. 环境概况

黄河流域环境变迁与该流域的地质条件、气候和人们的活动密切相关，大致分为蒙昧时期和文明时期。

（1）蒙昧时期的生态环境

自新石器时代开始，距今 8000—3000 年间是气候最好的时期，国外一般称为"气候适宜期"（Climatic Optimum）。这个第四纪冰期过后的温暖时期是对人类意义非凡的一段时期。在距今 5000 年前后，四大文明，苏美尔文明（两河流域）、古埃及文明（尼罗河流域）、哈拉帕文明（印度河-恒河流域）、华夏文明（黄河流域）差不多同时兴起。"当时全球各地的年平均温度普遍比现代高 2—3℃，西伯利亚的永久冻土带完全消失，代之而起的喜温湿的栎、榆、赤杨等组成的温带落叶阔叶林横贯亚欧大陆北部。"[1]亚热带气候基本上控制了黄河流域。与今天相比，亚热带气候向北差不多迁移了 2 个纬度以上。大约西起关中平原北缘，东渡黄河之后，顺延汾河谷地北上，斜贯山西高原，而后循永定河东去，直至渤海湾西岸，可称为亚热带北界。北京、天津正处于亚热带北缘，气候与今天的合肥、信阳、汉中相似。茂密的亚热带阔叶林、水蕨科植物、竹类相当普遍地分布于黄河中下游地区，喜热动物也出没其间。人们在西安半坡遗址中发现的水獐、竹鼠和貉等动物骨骼遗骸，在今天西安地区早已不复存在，而在现今长江流域的沼泽地带才能发现它们。出土的商代甲骨上的刻文记载了人们打猎时捕获大象的事实，这表明安阳一带至少在商代时已有大象活动。

由上可推知，黄河流域在 5000 年以前曾是生态优美的地域：气候温暖湿润，森林草原广布，绿野遍地、河湖纵横，动物出没其间。在肥沃的土壤上，我们的先民开始劳作，用双手开创了华夏文明的先河。

---

[1] 王会昌.中国文化地理[M].武汉：华中师范大学出版社，1992:37.

I. Environmental Changes in the Yellow River Basin

Environmental change in the Yellow River Basin is a long process dating back 10,000 years before.

1. Environmental Overview

Environmental changes in the Yellow River Basin are closely related to the geological conditions, climate and people's activities in the basin, which are roughly divided into the period of obscurity and the period of civilization.

(1) The Ecological Environment in the Period of Obscurity

Since the Neolithic period, the period between 8,000 to 3,000 years ago was the best climate period. This period is generally referred to as the Climatic Optimum in foreign countries. This period of warmth after the Quaternary Ice Age was a period of great significance to mankind. Around 5,000 years ago, four major civilizations emerged at about the same time: Sumerian (in Mesopotamia), Ancient Egyptian (in the Nile Basin), Harappan (in the Indus-Ganges Basin), and Chinese (in the Yellow River Basin). "At that time, the average temperature around the world is 2℃ to 3℃ higher than that of today. Siberian permafrost zone completely disappeared, replaced by moisture-loving oak elm, alder and other components of the temperate deciduous broad-leaved forests across the northern part of Eurasia".[1] The subtropical climate basically controlled the Yellow River Basin. Compared with today, the subtropical climate has moved northward by almost 2 degrees of latitude or more. It starts from the northern edge of Guanzhong Plain in the west, crosses the Yellow River in the east, follows the valley of Fen River in the north, slopes through the Shanxi Plateau, and then follows the Yongding River in the east to the west coast of Bohai Bay, which can be called the northern boundary of subtropics. Beijing and Tianjin are at the northern edge of the subtropics, and the climate is similar to that of Hefei, Xinyang and Hanzhong today. The dense subtropical broad-leaved forests, Parkeriaceae and bamboos are

---

[1] Wang Huichang. Cultural Geography of China [M]. Wuhan: Huazhong Normal University Press, 1992:37.

（2）文明时期的生态环境

生态系统的基础是植被，动物和微生物依此有了特殊的栖息环境。史念海教授认为黄河中游主要的植被类型是森林[1]，并系统研究了历史上黄河中游植被的变迁过程。这一过程大概分为四个时期：①春秋至战国时期。这一时期又可分为前后两个阶段。前一阶段显示黄河流域早期森林规模较大，植被覆盖率较高，裸露之地少。后一阶段，平原地区的森林逐渐被砍伐，到战国末期，平原的森林绝大部分遭到破坏，林区面积明显缩小。②平原地区森林破坏严重的时代。这一时代行将结束时，平原地区已基本上无森林可言。③山地森林严重破坏时期。这一时期，森林地区面积继续缩小，由于远程采伐范围不断扩大，山地森林受到比较严重的破坏。④森林受到摧残性破坏的时代。自明代中叶至清时，黄河中游地区的森林受到了摧残性破坏。陈永宗则认为：黄河中游尤其是黄土高原的主要植被类型是森林和草原，早期历史的森林覆盖率不可能达到53%，准确的划分应是森林草原带和草原带，森林主要分布在周围山地，历史上曾遭受了程度不同的多次破坏。[2] 尽管人们对黄河中游植被情况的研究结论不尽相同，但是，比较认同的观点是，由于大规模的人类活动，黄土高原的天然植被曾经遭受了毁灭性破坏。

黄河流域生态环境的变迁在河湖分布上也有较为显著的体现。远古时期黄河流域的湖泊如大陆泽、大野泽等集中分布于今河南、山东与河北接壤地区。据先秦文献统计有40多个，我们可以肯定，文献记载有不少遗漏。除下游外，中游地区同样分布有许多湖泊。汉唐时期影响河湖分布的自然因素变化并不激烈，平原地区的湖泊虽有淤浅趋势，但总体布局却没有发生根本性的变化。《水经注》中记载的湖泊沼泽超过

---

[1] 史念海.历史时期黄河中游的森林[M]//史念海.河山集：二集.太原：山西人民出版社，1999：322.

[2] 陈永宗.黄土高原现代侵蚀与治理[M].北京：科学出版社，1988.

quite common in the middle and lower reaches of the Yellow River, and heat-loving animals are also found in the area. The skeletal remains of water roe deer, bamboo rats and raccoon dogs found at the Banpo Site in Xi'an have long since disappeared from the Xi'an area and can only be found in the swampy areas of the present-day Yangtze River Basin. The fact that elephants were captured during hunting was recorded in the Shang oracle bones excavated, indicating that elephants were active in the Anyang area at least during the Shang Dynasty.

It can be deduced from the above that the Yellow River Basin was an area with beautiful ecological environment 5,000 years ago: the climate was warm and humid, forests and grasslands were widespread, green fields, rivers and lakes were everywhere, and animals were found in the fertile soil where our ancestors began to work and started the Chinese civilization with their hands.

(2) Ecological Environment in the Period of Civilization

The basis of the ecosystem is vegetation, which provides a special habitat for animals and microorganisms. Professor Shi Nianhai believes that the main vegetation type in the middle reaches of the Yellow River was forest[1], and has systematically studied the process of vegetation change in the middle reaches of the Yellow River throughout history. This process is roughly divided into four periods: ① Spring and Autumn to Warring States period. This period can be further divided into two phases: the early and the latter. In the first phase, the early forests in the Yellow River Basin were large in scale, with high vegetation cover and little bare land. In the latter stage, the forests in the plains were gradually cut down, and by the end of the Warring States period, most of the forests in the plains were destroyed and the forest area was obviously reduced. ② The era of severe forest destruction in the plains. At the end of this period, there were basically no forests left in the plain areas. ③ The period of severe destruction of mountain forests. During this period, the forest area continued to shrink, and the mountain forests were more severely damaged due to the expansion of remote logging. ④ The period of devastating destruction of forests. From the middle of the Ming Dynasty to the Qing Dynasty, the forests in the middle reaches of the

---

[1] Shi Nianhai. Forests in the middle reaches of the Yellow River during the historical period (Heshanji II) [M]. Taiyuan: Shanxi People's Publishing House, 1999:322.

500处,其中位于黄淮海平原上的湖沼有190多个,先秦时的湖泊在这一时期内基本尚存。[1]但是,唐以后黄河中游湖泊就逐渐干涸,下游湖泊淤浅状况更是明显。宋以后黄河中游已几乎没有湖泊存在,下游湖泊也发生根本性变化,众多湖泊淤为平陆。以开封为例,历史上早期,开封西北,黄河由大伾山折向北流,北面有济水东流,南濒汴水与淮泗相通,西有圃田泽,东南有逢泽,附近河湖交错。在战国前后,它是全国重要的经济都会,隋开通济渠,使开封成为漕运中心。中唐、五代时,开封水陆交通四通八达。北宋时,河湖已有较大的变化,但汴河漕运仍是京师的生命线。然而,随着气候干旱,水源短缺,汴河又因泥沙淤积致使通航条件逐渐丧失,到14世纪时,开封已经成为一个不通航的城市。

黄河小浪底水利枢纽工程
Yellow River Xiaolangdi Water Resources Hub Project

---

[1] 陈桥驿.水经注研究[M].天津:天津古籍出版社,1985:65-67.

Yellow River were devastated. Chen Yongzong, on the other hand, believes that: the main vegetation types of the middle reaches of the Yellow River, especially the Loess Plateau, were forests and grasslands. The forest coverage in the early history could not reach 53%, and the accurate division should be forest-steppe belt and grassland belt. Forests were mainly distributed in the surrounding mountains, which had been destroyed many times in different degrees throughout history. [1] Although people's research on the vegetation situation in the middle reaches of the Yellow River has come to different conclusions, the more agreed view is that the natural vegetation of the Loess Plateau had suffered devastating destruction due to large-scale human activities.

Changes in the ecological environment of the Yellow River Basin in the distribution of rivers and lakes are also quite obvious. In ancient times, the Yellow River Basin lakes such as the Dalu Lake, Daye Lake, etc. were concentratedly distributed in present-day Henan, Shandong and Hebei bordering areas. According to the pre-Qin literature, there were more than 40 such lakes. We can be sure that there are many omissions in the literature. In addition to the downstream, there were also many lakes distributed in the middle reaches. The natural factors affecting the distribution of rivers and lakes in the Han and Tang dynasties did not change drastically, and the overall layout of lakes in the plain area did not change fundamentally, although there was a trend of siltation and shallowing. There were more than 500 lakes and marshes recorded in the *Commentary of the Waterways Classic*, among which more than 190 lakes and marshes were located in the Yellow and Huaihai Plain, and the lakes of the pre-Qin Dynasty basically survived in this period. [2] However, after the Tang Dynasty, the lakes in the middle reaches of the Yellow River dried up gradually, and the siltation of the lakes in the lower reaches was even more obvious. After the Song Dynasty, there were almost no lakes in the middle reaches of the Yellow River, and the downstream lakes also underwent fundamental changes, with

---

[1] Chen Yongzong Modern Erosion and Treatment of the Loess Plateau [M]. Beijing: Science Press, 1988.

[2] Chen Qiaoyi. Studies on the Studies on the Commentary of the Waterways Classic [M]. Tianjin: Tianjin Ancient Books Publishing House, 1985:65-67.

2. 环境变迁主导因素

根据史料，分析主导黄河流域环境变迁的因素，可从以下两方面进行：

（1）气候波动影响生态植被

植被生长主要依赖气候条件，气候波动往往直接影响植被生长。黄河流域环境的变迁，一个重要原因就是气候的波动。而冷暖交替、干湿叠加是一个地区气候变化的基本规律。气候作为某一地区多年大气状况的平均值，温度（冷暖）、湿度（干湿）是人们描述大气状况的常用参数。受制于一些主要因子如太阳辐射、大气环流、下垫面的性质等影响，在自然状态下，气候会发生冷暖周期性波动。距今22亿年至1万年之间，地球上曾先后出现过三次大冰期。冰期期间，气温呈下降趋势；在间冰期，气温又呈上升趋势。在每次冰期或间冰期之间可能还会有小的波动。一般来说，人们对于历史时期（1万年以来）气候的波动知道得较为详细。例如，距今8000—3000年间的"气候适宜期"（前已述及）。由于缺乏量化的数据，有关前5000年的气候我们无法精确描述。不过，近5000年来的气候变化，竺可桢先生曾做了系统的研究，主要表现为冷暖交替出现（地质时期3个温暖期3个寒冷期，历史时期4个温暖期4个寒冷期），干湿叠加其上，成为冷干冷湿、暖湿暖干几种典型气候。[1]

气候的波动会影响生态植被，黄河中下游地区作为中华民族的发祥地之一，生态环境尤其是植被是气候作用的直接产物。温暖湿润的气候，往往带来风调雨顺，茂盛的植被，良好的生态环境；寒冷干燥的气候，又严重威胁植被的生长，甚至导致其死亡，随之而来的就是频繁的灾害。

（2）人类活动影响生态环境

气候状况又决定了人类活动的方式，尤其是耕作方式。自夏以来的3000年间，干旱半干旱温带气候控制黄河中游地区，在黄土高原上，天

---

[1] 竺可桢.中国近五千年来气候变迁的初步研究[J].考古学报，1972(1).

many lakes silting up to flat land. Take Kaifeng as an example, in the early history, northwest of Kaifeng, the Yellow River flowed northward from Dapi Mountain; Jishui River flowed eastward in the north; Bianshui River was connected with Huai-Si River in the south; Putian Lake in the west and Feng Lake in the southeast; and nearby rivers and lakes were intertwined. Before and after the Warring States period, it was an important economic capital of the country, and the Sui opened the Tongji Canal, making Kaifeng the center of transportation. During the middle Tang and Five Dynasties, Kaifeng was well connected with water and land transportation. In the Northern Song Dynasty, the rivers and lakes changed a lot, but Bianhe Canal was still the lifeline of the capital. However, with the dry climate and water shortage, Bianhe River gradually lost its navigable condition due to siltation. By the 14th century, Kaifeng had become a non-navigable city.

2. Leading Factors of Environmental Change

According to the historical data, the dominant factors of environmental changes in the Yellow River Basin can be analyzed from the following two aspects.

(1) Climate Fluctuations Affect Ecological Vegetation

Vegetation growth is mainly dependent on climate conditions, and climate fluctuations often directly affect vegetation growth. An important reason for the environmental changes in the Yellow River Basin is the fluctuation of climate. The alternation of cold and warmth, accompanied by diverse humidity, is the basic law of climate change in a region. Climate is the average of atmospheric conditions in a certain area over many years. Temperature (warm and cold), humidity (wet and dry) are the common parameters that people use to describe the atmospheric conditions. Due to the influence of some major factors such as solar radiation, atmospheric circulation, and the nature of the subsurface, climate undergoes periodic fluctuations of warm and cold in its natural state. During the period of 2.2 billion to 10,000 years ago, there were three recurrent major ice ages on Earth. During an ice age, the temperature tends to fall; during an interglacial period, the temperature tends to rise again. There may also be small fluctuations between each ice age or interglacial period. In general, the fluctuations in climate over the historical period (10,000 years to the present) are known in some detail, such as

黄河口生长繁茂的适生草木（侯全亮摄）

the "period of climatic suitability" between 8,000 to 3,000 years ago (mentioned above). Due to the lack of quantitative data, it is not possible to describe the climate of the first 5,000 years precisely. However, the climate change in the last 5,000 years has been systematically studied by Mr. Zhu Kezhen and is mainly characterized by the alternation of cold and warm periods (3 warm periods and 3 cold periods in the geological period, 4 warm periods and 4 cold periods in the historical period) with dry and wet superimposed on them, which become several typical climates of cold dry, cold wet, warm wet and warm dry. [1]

The fluctuation of climate will affect the ecological vegetation. The middle and lower reaches of the Yellow River region as one of the birthplaces of the Chinese people, ecological environment, especially vegetation is a direct product of climate action. Warm and humid climate, often brings wind and rain, lush vegetation, good ecological environment. A cold and dry climate, in turn, seriously threatens the growth of vegetation and even causes its death, and consequently, disasters are frequent.

(2) Human Activities Affect the Ecological Environment

Climate conditions in turn determine the way of human activities, especially farming. For 3,000 years since the Xia Dynasty, the arid and semi-arid temperate climate controlled the middle reaches of the Yellow River. On the Loess Plateau, the natural vegetation was mostly temperate forest steppe and grassland landscape. In accordance with the laws of nature, human activities should be mainly pastoralism. Based on the analysis of historical documents, Zhu Shiguang et al. have studied the geographical distribution of agricultural (farming) and pastoral (non-farming) areas in the early Loess Plateau region and have drawn general maps of the distribution in different periods. By superimposing these maps, we can see the moving status of the boundary line between farming and non-farming areas, and the Loess Plateau is the oscillating area of this boundary line. When the Loess Plateau is a non-farming area, a large area of land becomes grassland or shrubs or sparse forest, and soil and water conservation is good, and the erosion intensity of the watershed is low. When part or all of it is an agricultural area, the

---

[1] Zhu Kezhen. A preliminary study of climate change in China in the last 5,000 years[J]. Journal of Archaeology, 1972(1).

然植被多是温带森林草原和草原景观。顺应自然规律，人类活动方式应以牧业为主。朱士光等曾以历史文献分析为基础，研究了早期黄土高原地区农业区（农耕）和牧业区（非农耕）的地理分布，并绘制了不同时期的分布概图。把这些图幅加以叠加，可以看到农耕区与非农耕区的分界线移动状况，黄土高原是这一界线的摆动区域。当黄土高原是非农耕区时，大片土地成为草场或灌木、疏林，水土保持较好，流域侵蚀强度低。当部分或全部是农耕区时，植被遭到破坏，水土流失严重。其中的变化原因，可以从三个方面加以分析：①农耕文化优于游牧文化。农耕世界的范围不断扩大，这是世界历史的发展趋势。②人口增加需要更多耕地。为了生存，必须开垦更多的土地，而农牧交错地带则是开垦的首选之地。③巩固边防需要屯田。政府实行屯田制，把森林草原开垦为耕地。

vegetation is destroyed and soil erosion is serious. The reasons for this change can be analyzed from three aspects: ①Farming culture is better than nomadic culture. The farming world is expanding, which is the trend of world history. ②The increase in population required more arable land. In order to survive, more land had to be reclaimed, and the intersection of agriculture and pastoralism was the first place to do so. ③Consolidation of border defense required garrisons to be self-sufficient in food production. The government implemented the army farming system to reclaim the forest and grassland as farmland.

二、历史上黄河流域的洪涝灾害及防治

黄河是中华民族的母亲河，也是一条多灾多难的河。它的灾害主要是水灾。黄河流域降水量很少，平均每年只有400毫米，但是黄河流域每年降水量的一半左右经常集中在夏季的七八月份，这种夏季集中的暴雨，经常造成黄河洪水暴涨，称为"伏汛"。黄河的水灾大部分是这种夏季暴雨造成的，此外，有时九十月间，也可能有大雨造成洪水，称为"秋汛"。三四月间，冰雪融化也常引起洪水，称为"桃汛"。黄河在甘肃、内蒙古边境和山东境内是由南向北流的，在南部化冰的季节，北部往往还在封冻，大量流冰在下游被阻，壅塞河道，也会造成河水暴涨，称为"凌汛"。

黄河的水灾之所以特别严重，不仅因为黄河流域的夏季暴雨，更重要的还是由于黄河下游的泥沙淤积。黄河的含沙量在世界各国的河流中占第一位，年平均输沙量约16亿吨。黄河泥沙到了下游后，因河道平缓，泥沙不能完全入海而大量沉积，河道就逐年淤浅，直至高出河堤两旁的地面，成为"地上河"。中下游河床越抬越高，遇到较大的洪水，河堤无法约束的时候，黄河下游就要发生泛滥、决口等严重灾害。

根据黄河水利委员会所编的《人民黄河》的统计，在1946年以前的三四千年中，黄河决口泛滥达1593次，其中明代决口就达456次，平均约每7个月一次；从清初到鸦片战争（1644—1840年）近200年间，决口达361次，平均每6个多月一次。较大的改道有26次，其中明代大改道7次，清代1次，民国时期1次。改道最北的一度汇入海河，经大沽口入海。改道最南的一度经淮河汇入长江，最后由江入海。

就河流变迁大势而言，在宋室南迁之后，自河南开封而东，河势渐趋东南，由淮河入黄海。元末，顺帝至正四年（1344年），黄河在山东曹县西南的白茅堤决口北流，侵及山东东平西南的安山，北沿会通河，

II. The History of the Yellow River Basin Floods and Prevention

The Yellow River is the mother river of the Chinese nation, but also a disaster-prone river. Its disasters are mainly floods. The Yellow River Basin has very little rainfall, only 400mm of rainfall per year on average, but about half of the annual rainfall in the Yellow River Basin is often concentrated in the summer months of July and August. This kind of concentrated heavy rainfall in summer often causes the Yellow River floods, which is called "Summer Floods". Most of the floods in the Yellow River are caused by this summer rainfall. In addition, sometimes in September and October, there may also be floods caused by heavy rain, called "Autumn Floods". In March and April, the melting of snow and ice also often causes floods, called "Peach Floods". The Yellow River in Gansu, Inner Mongolia border and Shandong is flowing from the south to the north. When the ice in the south starts to melt, the north is often still frozen. A large amount of ice in the downstream is blocked in the river, which will also cause floods, called "Ice Floods".

The flooding of the Yellow River is particularly serious not only because of the heavy summer rains in the Yellow River Basin, but more importantly because of the siltation of the lower Yellow River. The sand content of the Yellow River is the highest in the world's rivers, with an average annual sand transport of about 1.6 billion tons. When the sediment comes to the lower reaches, it cannot be carried by the flow into the sea due to the gentle streamway, so the river will be silted up year by year, until higher than the ground on both sides of the riverbank, and become "a Hanging River". The riverbed in the middle and lower reaches of the river is getting higher and higher, and when a larger flood occurs and the riverbank cannot be restrained, a serious disaster will occur in the lower reaches of the Yellow River in the form of a breach or flood.

According to the statistics of *Yellow River* compiled by the Yellow River Water Conservancy Commission, in the three or four thousand years before 1946, the Yellow River broke flooding 1,593 times, including 456 times in the Ming Dynasty, an average of about once every 7 months; in the 200 years from

东注清济河，分两股向河北的河间和山东的济南一带注入渤海。而元朝统治者每年需从江南一带运送漕米二三百万石至北京，黄河改道北流，就破坏了南北运河的运粮航道。为了改善漕运，至正十一年（1351年），朝廷征民夫15万，调戍军2万，派贾鲁治河，使黄河回归故道，即由归德（今河南商丘地区）东经徐州合泗水，南流到淮阴汇入黄河。这就是后人所说的"贾鲁故道"。

明朝先后出现7次大改道，分别是明太祖洪武二十四年（1391年）、明成祖永乐十四年（1416年）、明英宗正统十三年（1448年）、明孝

黄河南岸（王伟摄）

the beginning of the Qing Dynasty to the Opium War (1644 -1840), 361 times, an average of once every six months. There were 26 major diversions, including seven major diversions in the Ming Dynasty, one in the Qing Dynasty and one in the Republic of China Period. The northernmost diversion once merged into the Haihe River and entered the sea through the Dagukou. And the southeast diversion made the Yellow River merge into the Yangtze River through Huaihe River, and finally enter the sea.

In terms of river changes, after the Song Dynasty moved south, from the east of Kaifeng, Henan Province, the Yellow River tends to southeast, converging into the Huaihe River and then flows into the Yellow Sea. At the end of the Yuan Dynasty, in the fourth year of Emperor Shun (1344), the Yellow River broke its mouth at Baimao Dike, southwest of Cao County in Shandong, flowing northward and invading Anshan, southwest of Dongping in Shandong. In the north the Yellow River flows along the Huitong River, in the east into the Qingji River, and respectively flow to Hejian in Hebei and Jinan in Shandong, and finally into the Bohai Sea. The rulers of the Yuan Dynasty needed to transport two or three million stones of rice from Jiangnan to Beijing every year, when the Yellow River was diverted to the north, it destroyed the north and south canals of the grain transport channel. In order to improve the transport, in the eleventh year of Zhizheng (1351), the court levied 150,000 people, 20,000 garrison troops, and sent Jia Lu to regulate the river, making the Yellow River back to the old course, that is, from Gui De (present Shangqiu area in Henan Province), to Sishui River in Xuzhou in the east, then joined the Yellow River in Huaiyin in the south. This is what later people call "Jia Lu Old Course".

The seven major diversions that occurred during the Ming Dynasty were in the 24th year of the reign of Emperor Taizu(1391), the 14th year of the reign of Emperor Chengzu(1416), the 13th year of the reign of Emperor Yingzong(1448), the 2nd year of the reign of Emperor Xiaozong(1489), the 4th year of the reign of Empeor Wuzong(1509), the 13th year(1534) and the 37th year (1558)of the reign of Emperor Shizong . In the 15th year of Chongzhen (1642), the Ming rulers dug through Zhujiazhai on the south bank of the Yellow River in order to drown the peasant uprising of Li Zicheng. Flood waters rushed into Kaifeng City, drowning 340,000 of the city's 370,000 inhabitants and causing a great tragedy that almost

宗弘治二年（1489年）、明武宗正德四年（1509年）、明世宗嘉靖十三年（1534年）、明世宗嘉靖三十七年（1558年）。崇祯十五年（1642年），明统治者为了淹没李自成农民起义军，掘开黄河南岸朱家寨，洪水冲进开封城，将城内37万居民淹死34万，造成几乎全城覆没的大悲剧。

明末河决开封，决口尚未堵合而明已亡。清顺治元年（1644年）堵塞决口后，黄河回归故道，由开封经河南兰考、商丘、虞城，山东曹县、单县，安徽砀山、江苏丰县、沛县、萧县、徐州、灵璧、睢宁、邳县、宿迁、泗阳，在淮阴与淮河汇合，经云梯关入海。后经康熙、雍正、乾隆三代的治理，黄河两岸堤坝渐趋完整，虽然两岸还不断决口，但都进行了堵合，直到咸丰五年（1855年）以前，未再发生过大的改道。

由于明末清初连续40多年的战乱，黄河堤防失修，在顺治执政的18年（1644—1661年）中，黄河决口即有八九个年头之多（《清史稿·河渠志》）。其中数次北决，漕运受到很大影响。因此，清初即确定了治河与保漕通盘筹划的方针。当时维持漕运有两大威胁：一是黄河改道使漕运中断，因为黄河从徐州至清河段也是运河的一段。二是黄河决口冲淤山东境内的运河。这就决定了黄河必须走"南道"，而且豫东及鲁苏北堤的防御和江苏境内黄河段是治理的重点。对漕运而言还有两个关键点：清口与高家堰。清口是黄、淮交汇处，淮水至此大部分汇黄入海，小部分南流补给江北运河。因黄河的顶托及高家堰大堤的拦蓄作用，洪泽湖逐渐扩大，淮河与之相合，清口成为洪泽湖的主要出口。而黄河多沙，若清口淤塞，则漕运受阻，洪泽湖亦排泄不利，将导致湖水蓄水量大增，转而威胁湖东高家堰大堤的安全。如高家堰溃决，不仅为患苏北，阻碍漕运，而且洪泽湖不能储蓄淮河清水，又失去借清水冲刷清口和黄河淤泥的作用。为了实现治河、导淮、济运三种目的，清朝历代对淮安、清口一带的治理无不给予了高度关注。

进入民国时期，军阀混战，民不聊生，黄河洪涝灾害时有发生。尤其是1933年8月黄河陕县发生特大洪水，黄河在河南温县决口，从温

wiped out the whole city.

At the end of the Ming Dynasty, the Yellow River broke at Kaifeng, and the Dynasty fell before the mouth could be blocked. After blocking the breach in the first year of Shunzhi in the Qing Dynasty (1644), the Yellow River returned to its old course, passing from Kaifeng, Lankao, Shangqiu and Yucheng in Henan, Caoxian and Shanxian in Shandong, Dangshan in Anhui, Fengxian, Peixian, Xiaoxian, Xuzhou, Lingbi, Suining, Pixian, Suqian and Siyang in Jiangsu, and merging with the Huai he River in Huaiyin and then into the sea at Yuntiguan. After the governance of three emperors—Kangxi, Yongzheng, Qianlong, the Yellow River embankment was gradually completed, and although breaches still occured, they were blocked in time, and no major diversions occurred until the fifth year of Xianfeng in the Qing Dynasty (1855).

The Yellow River embankments fell into disrepair as a result of more than 40 consecutive years of warfare in the late Ming and early Qing dynasties. In the 18 years of Shunzhi's reign (1644-1661), there were eight or nine years of breakdowns, as shown in the *Qing Historical Manuscript - River and Drainage Records*. The canal was greatly affected by several of these northern breakdowns. As a result, the early Qing Dynasty established a policy of overall planning for the management of the river and the preservation of the canal. At that time, there were two major threats to the maintenance of the canal: one was the diversion of the Yellow River, which interrupted the canal, as the Yellow River from Xuzhou to Qinghe was also a section of the canal. Secondly, the Yellow River's breach washed away the canal in Shandong. This dictated that the Yellow River had to take the "southern route" and that the defiance of the riverbanks in eastern Henan, Shandong, northern Jiangsu and the Yellow River in Jiangsu were the main focus of treatment. There were two other key points for water transport: Qingkou and Gaojiayan. Qingkou was the meeting point between the Yellow River and the Huai he River, where most of the Huai he water flowed into the sea after merging with the Yellow River and a small part flowed south to replenish the canals north of the river. Due to the support of the Yellow River and the impounding effect of the Gaojiayan embankment, Hongze Lake gradually expanded and the Huai he River merged with it, making Qingkou the main outlet of Hongze Lake . As the Yellow River was sandy, if Qingkou was blocked, transport would be impeded

县到河北长垣（今属河南）间200多千米的堤段内，决口达50余处之多，汇成五股，南北分流，淹没冀鲁豫等省67县1.2万平方千米土地，受灾人口364万，死亡1.8万余人。1935年，黄河又在山东鄄城决口，害及苏北。1938年，国民党军在河南郑州附近挖开黄河南岸花园口大堤，造成黄河大改道，受灾面积5.4万平方千米，千百万人流离失所，死亡89万人，豫东、皖北、苏北的广大平原一片汪洋，灾情之重，为以往之罕见。

近代以来，由于西方科学技术的引进，进步的知识分子积极把近代科技与黄河治理的实际状况相结合，逐步开展了一些基础性工作，促进了治理黄河方略的发展，如基本资料的观测、收集和河流治理的规划研究等。李仪祉、张含英等人提出了系统治理黄河的主张，开始研究水流和泥沙的来源和规律，对于水温观测和地形测量做了一些工作，并运用到黄河的上游、中游和支流上去，但是由于当时帝国主义的侵略、政治腐败、经济困难等原因，治理黄河的实际工作没有什么进展，特别是在国民党反动统治时代，黄河危害更甚。

1945年8月，日军投降后，国民党政府即做出了堵塞花园口、引黄河回归故道的决定。1946年2月，国民党政府成立黄河堵口复堤工程局，并且立即进行堵口的准备工作。国民党政府的这一举动立即引起了国际和国内社会各界的极大关注。中国共产党以国家大局为重，同意黄河归故，但由于这一举动对冀鲁豫解放区关系重大，遂明确提出了先复堤后堵口的正确主张，而国民党政府无意复堤，积极堵口，妄图水淹解放区，以达到其以水代兵的军事企图。为此，中国共产党在一年多的时间内同国民党政府在堵口、复堤以及费用等方面进行了极其尖锐的政治、经济和军事的斗争。中国共产党采取了正确、灵活的方针，经过艰苦的谈判，为解放区赢得了80亿元的工程款和150亿元的救济费及大量的治河工程物资，同时，推迟堵口工程达9个月之久，为我解放区人民进行大规模培土复堤争取了时间，为粉碎国民党的阴谋，保证黄河安澜做出了重要贡献。

and Hongze Lake would not be able to drain, leading to a large increase in water storage, which would in turn threaten the safety of the Gaojiayan embankment on the east of the lake. If Gaojiayan embankment collapsed, not only would it be a problem for northern Jiangsu and impede transport, but Hongze Lake would not be able to save the clear water of the Huai he River and would lose its role in flushing out the siltation of Qingkou and the Yellow River. In order to achieve the three purposes of river management, that is, the Yellow River management, Huai he River guidance and water transport improvement, the Qing Dynasty had paid great attention to the management of Huai'an and Qingkou area.

Entering the period of the Republic of China, the warlords were at war and the people were in desperate straits, and flooding of the Yellow River occurred from time to time. In particular, in August 1933, the Yellow River broke in Shaan County, Henan Province, with more than 50 breaches in a 200-kilometre section of the embankment from Wen County to Changyuan (now part of Henan Province) north of the river, forming five streams and diverting north and south, flooding 12,000 square kilometers of land in 67 counties in Hebei, Shandong and Henan provinces, affecting 3.64 million people and killing 18,000. In 1935, the Yellow River burst its banks in Juancheng, Shandong, the damage even extended to northern Jiangsu. In 1938, the National Government of the Republic of China exploded Huayuankou embankment, the southern bank of the Yellow River, near Zhengzhou, Henan Province, causing a major diversion, which affected 54,000 square kilometers with millions of displaced people and caused 890,000 deaths. The vast plains of eastern Henan, northern Anhui, and northern Jiangsu were ruined by flood, and the disaster was so severe that it was rarely seen in the past.

In modern times, due to the introduction of Western science and technology, progressive intellectuals actively combined modern technology with the actual situation of the Yellow River management, and gradually carried out some basic work, which promoted the development of the management strategy, such as the observation and collection of basic information and the planning and studies of river management, etc. Li Yizhi, Zhang Hanying etc. put forward the idea of systematic management of the Yellow River, and began to study the sources and patterns of water flow and sediment, and did some work on water temperature observations and topographic surveys, which were applied to the upper, middle

092　　第三章　黄河流域水利工程对生态保护的意义

三门峡激水（王伟摄）

and tributary reaches of the Yellow River, but due to imperialist aggression, political corruption and economic difficulties at the time, little progress was made in the practical management of the Yellow River, especially during the reactionary reign of Kuomintang, which made it even more dangerous.

After the Japanese army surrendered in August 1945, the Kuomintang government made the decision to block the Huayuankou breach and return the Yellow River to its former course, and in February 1946, it set up the Yellow River Blocking and Dike Restoration Project Bureau and immediately made preparations for the blocking. This move by the Kuomintang government immediately aroused great concern among the international and domestic communities. The Chinese Communist Party agreed to return the Yellow River to its former course in the interest of the nation. However, since this move was of great importance to the CPC liberated areas of Hebei, Shandong and Henan, the correct idea of restoring the dike before blocking the breach was clearly put forward. The Kuomintang government had no intention of restoring the dike and actively blocked the breach with a vain attempt to flood the CPC liberated areas in order to achieve its military intention of using flood as weapon. To this end, the CPC engaged in an extremely sharp political, economic and military struggle with the Kuomintang government for more than a year over the blocking of the banks, the restoration of the dike and the costs. After arduous negotiations, thanks to the correct and flexible approach adopted by the CPC, it was able to win 8 billion yuan for the project and 15 billion yuan for relief and a large amount of materials for the river control project for the liberated areas. At the same time, the postponement of the mouth-blocking project for nine months bought time for the people of CPC liberated areas to carry out large-scale soil cultivation and dike restoration and made an extremely important contribution to the CPC's efforts to smash the Kuomintang's plot and ensure the safety of the Yellow River.

It has been the wish of the people of the Yellow River for generations to make it work for the benefit of the Chinese people. After the founding of the PRC, the ancient Yellow River ushered in the spring of management and development. Under the leadership of the central government of the the PRC, various regions gradually went from sub-district management to unified management and carried out huge projects to repair and defend the Yellow River. In 1951, for example, for

让黄河为中华民族造福，是历代黄河儿女的美好愿望。新中国成立后，古老的黄河迎来了治理开发的春天。在中央政府的领导下，各地由分区治理逐渐走上统一治理，并进行了巨大的黄河修防工程，以1951年政府对治理黄河的投资为例，仅工程费一项就达5亿斤小麦之价值，比国民党统治时期最好的年份还超过57倍；1952年，在黄河堤防工程方面，培修了1300余千米的大堤，完成土方工程8200余万立方米，下游数以万计的坝埽全部由秸埽改为石坝，完成了石方工程170余万立方米。到1954年，人民政府在下游培修了黄河1800千米，完成土方1.3亿立方米；将原有保护堤坡的坝埽由秸料全部换成石料，共用石料230万立方米；在大堤上用锥探的方法发现了8万个洞穴和裂缝，全部加以填补，从根本上加固了堤防。[1]

新中国成立以后，人民治黄掀开了新的一页。虽然有几次黄河大洪水，但是在中国共产党的坚强领导下，未出现决口等重大灾情。

---

[1] 王瑞芳.当代中国水利史（1949—2011）[M].北京：中国社会科学出版社，2014:215-219.

the new government's investment in the management of the Yellow River, only the cost of the project amounted to 500 million *jin* of wheat, 57 times greater than that of the best year of the Kuomintang period; In 1952, in the Yellow River embankment project, more than 1,300 kilometers of dikes were built, more than 82 million m³ of earthworks completed. In downstream areas, tens of thousands of dams built with stalks were replaced with stone dams, more than 1.7 million m³ of stone works were completed. By 1954, the People's Government had repaired and reinforced 1,800 kilometers along the Yellow River in the downstream area, completed 130 million m³ of earthworks; The original dams protecting the embankment slopes built with stalks were all replaced with stone, using a total of 2.3 million m³ of stone; 80,000 holes and cracks were found on the embankment by cone probing and all were filled; therefore the embankment was fundamentally reinforced. [1]

After the founding of the PRC, a new page was opened in the regulation of the Yellow River by the people. Although there were several floods in the Yellow River, under the strong leadership of the Communist Party of China, there were no major disasters such as breakdowns.

---

[1] Wang Ruifang. The History of Contemporary Chinese Water Resources (1949-2011) [M]. China Social Science Press, 2014:215-219.

三、黄河流域水利枢纽工程与生态环境

新中国成立以来,黄河流域已建成龙羊峡、李家峡、刘家峡、青铜峡、龙口、三门峡、小浪底等十余座水利水电枢纽工程,流域水资源的开发利用率已达70%。其中,龙羊峡、刘家峡、三门峡、小浪底是具有综合效益的大型水利枢纽工程,这些工程在防洪、灌溉、供水等方面发挥了重要作用,改善了生态环境质量,而且开发了黄河的水电资源,获得了巨大的经济效益。

三门峡水利枢纽工程
Sanmenxia Water Conservancy Hub Project

河南省境内的三门峡、小浪底水利枢纽工程是黄河下游防洪工程体系的重要组成部分,对减少黄河下游河道淤积起到了保障作用。另外,这两个工程把黄河下游的防洪标准提高到了千年一遇的水平,保障了整个下游防洪工程体系运用的可靠性。小浪底水利枢纽投入运营以来,黄河连续23年不断流,完成多次引黄济津、引黄济青、引黄济淀等跨流域应急调水任务;还实现了黄河下游连续23年安全度汛,基本解除了黄河下游凌汛威胁;有效改善了小浪底库区和下游地区的生态环境。在

III. The Yellow River Basin Water Resources Hub Projects and the Ecological Environment

Since the founding of the PRC, more than ten water conservancy and hydropower hub projects have been built in the Yellow River Basin, including Longyangxia, Lijiaxia, Liujiaxia, Qingtongxia, Longkou, Sanmenxia and Xiaolangdi. Among them, Longyangxia, Liujiaxia, Sanmenxia and Xiaolangdi are large water conservancy hub projects with comprehensive benefits. These projects have played an important role in flood control, irrigation and water supply, improved the quality of the ecological environment, and have developed the hydropower resources of the Yellow River, reaping huge economic benefits.

The Sanmenxia and Xiaolangdi water conservancy hub projects in Henan Province are an important part of the lower reaches of the Yellow River flood control engineering system and have played a safeguard role in reducing river siltation in the lower reaches of the Yellow River. In addition, these two projects have raised the flood control standard of the lower reaches of the Yellow River to a once in about 1,000 years level, improving the reliability of the operation of the entire downstream flood control engineering system. Since the Xiaolangdi Water Conservancy Hub was put into operation, the Yellow River has been flowing continuously for 23 years, completing many inter-basin emergency water transfer tasks such as diverting the Yellow River to Tianjin, Qingdao and Baiyangdian,etc. It has also achieved 23 consecutive years of safe flooding in the lower reaches of the Yellow River and basically removed the threat of ice flood in the lower reaches; it has effectively improved the ecological environment in the Xiaolangdi reservoir area and downstream areas. In terms of ecological construction, water flow is regulated through the use of the Sanmenxia and Xiaolangdi water conservancy hub projects to reduce flood peaks when floods come and to counteract the impact of floods on the ecosystem; and to increase water flow during droughts and shortages, promoting the healthy development of the Yellow River Basin ecosystem. In 2000, the incoming water in the Yellow River Basin was significantly reduced and the lower reaches of the Yellow River were once again in danger of drying up. In this serious situation, the Xiaolangdi Reservoir project

生态建设方面，通过利用三门峡、小浪底水利枢纽工程来调节水流量，洪水来临时削减洪峰，抵御洪涝灾害对生态系统的冲击；干旱缺水时增加水流量，促进黄河流域生态系统的健康发展。2000年黄河流域来水明显减少，黄河下游又一次面临断流的危险。在这种严重的情况下，小浪底水库工程牺牲了自身的经济效益，停止发电，优先向下游提供生态用水，使得黄河下游在极其干旱的不利形势下，没有发生断流，从而使河口地区极其脆弱的生态系统得到了支撑和维持。

另外，在下游地区生态状况和调节生态用水方面，水库蓄水后，为沿岸地区居民的生活用水提供了便利条件，改善了黄河两岸自然生态环境，对实现黄河两岸的退耕还林、还草具有积极的推动作用。三门峡水库是黄河上修建的第一座以防洪、防凌、供水、灌溉、发电为目标的大型综合水利枢纽工程。工程建成后，从流域综合治理入手，通过实施拦、蓄、排、灌等遏制增量工程措施和植树种草生物措施，减少水土流失和污染程度，有效遏制进入黄河的泥沙和污染物；以三门峡库区清淤为突破口，紧紧抓住水沙关系调节这个"牛鼻子"，通过持续清淤，减少黄河泥沙的存量；以矿山生态修复，复耕复绿为重点，增加沿黄生态容量。牢固树立"一盘棋"思想，坚持共同抓好大保护，协同推进大治理，持续持久地开展山水林田湖草沙综合治理，这不仅有利于吸引更多野生动物，丰富生物多样性，而且有利于河岸稳固与水土保持，对工程起到一定的保护作用。几十年来，我们通过对水库的调节，为黄河下游防洪防凌安全、沿黄城市工业和农业用水、下游河道及河口地区生态平衡等，做出了巨大贡献，形成了依托水库发展的社会经济模式，形成了独特的生态系统和自然环境。黄河水变清了，气候变湿润了，形成较为优良的小气候条件，极大改善了两岸生态环境和用水条件。这种局部气候和当地栽培结构的改变，是维持区域生态平衡的最基本要素，三门峡库区湿地成为国家级珍禽动物白天鹅、鹤的越冬栖息地，已被国务院批准为国家级湿地自然保护区，几万只白天鹅及几十种鸟类在此越冬、栖息。库

sacrificed its own economic benefits by stopping power generation and giving priority to providing ecological water to the lower reaches of the river, allowing the lower reaches of the Yellow River to remain unbroken in an extremely dry and unfavorable situation, thus supporting and maintaining the extremely fragile ecosystem in the estuary.

In addition, in terms of ecological condition and regulation of ecological water in the downstream area, the reservoir storage provides convenient conditions for the living water of the residents, improves the natural ecological environment, and has a positive role in promoting the realization of the return of farmland to forest and grass on both sides of the Yellow River. Sanmenxia Reservoir is the first large comprehensive water conservancy hub project built on the Yellow River with the objectives of flood control, ice flood control, water supply, irrigation and power generation. After the completion of the project, starting from the comprehensive management of the watershed, through the implementation of interception, storage, drainage, irrigation and other measures to curb the increment and biological measures such as planting trees and grasses to reduce soil erosion and pollution and effectively curb the sediment and pollutants entering the Yellow River. Taking the dredging of Sanmenxia reservoir area as a breakthrough, we should hold tightly to the key of regulating the water-sand relationship and reduce the stock of Yellow River sediment through continuous dredging. We should focus on the ecological restoration of mines and replanting and greening to increase the ecological capacity along the Yellow River. We should firmly establish the idea of considering the overall situation, insist on jointly grasping the big protection, collaborate to promote the big governance, and continuously and persistently carry out comprehensive management of mountains, water, forests, farmlands, lakes, grasses and sands. This will not only help to attract more wildlife and enrich biodiversity, but also help to stabilize river banks and soil conservation, and play a protective role in the protection of the project. Over the past few decades, through the regulation of reservoirs, we have made great contributions to the safety of flood prevention, ice flood prevention, industrial and agricultural water use in cities along the Yellow River, and ecological balance in the downstream river and estuary, forming a socio-economic model that relies on reservoir development, forming a unique ecosystem and natural environment. The

区已形成的生态平衡，对调节地区气候、保护当地生物多样性及生态平衡，起着非常重要的作用。

三门峡天鹅湖国家城市湿地公园
Sanmenxia Swan Lake National Urban Wetland Park

　　由于中国历史上饱受洪涝、干旱之苦，人们赋予水利建设的任务主要是防洪、供水和灌溉，其中的供水也只是满足城镇生活和工业生产的基本需要，对生态用水问题考虑不足。如今这些问题已经引起重视，并不断得到改进。小浪底水库区为峡谷河段，有利于保持较大的长期有效库容，可以长期发挥调水调沙、兴利除害的效益，防洪运用比较可靠，不仅可以拦蓄特大洪水，还可以根据下游防洪需要适当控制中小型洪水。小浪底的泥沙处理方案，影响着下游河道水流发展趋势与河道形态变化，影响下游的生态环境。

　　黄河流域水资源的开发利用主要靠水利工程，水利工程的建设要与生态保护和生态环境建设相适应，要加强生态建设和环境保护，真正体现生态效益、经济效益、社会效益的统筹兼顾；将水利水电建设与生态环境密切结合起来，促进黄河流域水利水电开发与生态环境的综合治理，促进人与自然的和谐共生，维持黄河的健康发展。

Yellow River water becomes clearer, the climate becomes wetter, forming a more excellent microclimate conditions, greatly improving the ecological environment and water conditions on both sides. This change in local climate and local cultivation structure is the most essential element in maintaining the ecological balance of the region. Sanmenxia reservoir wetland has become a wintering habitat for national precious birds, such as mute swans and cranes, and has been approved by the State Council as a national wetland nature reserve, where tens of thousands of mute swans and dozens of other bird species roost in winter. The ecological balance that has developed in the reservoir plays an indispensable role in regulating the regional climate and protecting local biodiversity and ecological balance.

As China has historically suffered from floods and droughts, the task given to water conservancy construction was mainly flood control, water supply and irrigation, of which water supply was only to meet the basic needs of town life and industrial production, with insufficient consideration given to ecological water issues. Today these issues have been taken seriously and are constantly being improved. The Xiaolangdi reservoir area is a gorge section, which is conducive to maintaining a large long-term effective reservoir capacity and can play a long-term role in water and sand transfer, profit promotion and harm elimination, as well as in flood control. The Xiaolangdi sediment treatment scheme affects the downstream river flow development trend and changes in river morphology, influencing the downstream ecological environment.

The development and utilization of water resources in the Yellow River Basin mainly relies on water conservancy projects, the construction of which should be compatible with ecological protection and ecological environment construction, and should strengthen ecological construction and environmental protection, truly reflecting the co-ordination of ecological benefits, economic benefits and social benefits; we should closely integrate the construction of water conservancy and hydropower with the ecological environment, promote the comprehensive management of water conservancy and hydropower development and ecological environment in the Yellow River Basin, promote the harmonious coexistence of man and nature, and maintain the healthy development of the Yellow River.

四、水利工程归根到底是生态工程

　　黄河流域水少沙多，大部分属于干旱半干旱地区，多年平均降水量为 400 多毫米。1919 年至 1975 年黄河多年平均天然径流量为 580 亿立方米。20 世纪 90 年代以来，随着黄河流域人口急剧增长和不适当的人类活动，黄河连年发生断流，下游河道严重萎缩，过洪能力急剧下降；水流自净能力衰退，水体污染严重，流域生态环境压力越来越大。

　　设计修建水利工程的根本目的，就是对水资源进行综合利用，变害为利，根本上就是生态工程。要把工程目标进行拓展，要加大对水资源的节约、保护和合理配置的力度，不仅重视经济效益，更要注重生态效益，时时刻刻发挥水利工程的生态功能，从而使水利工程更好地适应现代社会的需要。一些人认为，水电是清洁廉价的能源，应最大限度地加以开发利用，不应让河水白白地流掉。而实际上，由于水电开发造成的对原生生态环境和水环境难以恢复的破坏，它已很难被称为是"清洁"的了。另外，水也并不是"白白地"在河里流，它是生态资源存在的一种形式，当仅仅从单一的经济利益出发，就会出现对水资源的过度开发与低效利用，从而破坏维持河流生命和生态系统的合理资源储存，最终将遭到大自然的报复和惩罚。

　　黄河是中华民族的母亲河，几千年来多灾多难。新中国建立以来的伟大治黄实践使她迎来了新生。尤其是小浪底水利枢纽工程的建成使用，发挥了重要的生态效益。它除了实现防洪、减淤的目标，还兼顾了发电和下游供水、灌溉等综合功能，同时提高了下游 4000 万亩耕地的灌溉用水保证，为黄河沿岸城乡生产、生活、生态用水提供了有力支撑。下游的河南、山东连续数年大旱仍能获得丰收，就是生态环境改善的最直接明证。水库对库区环境改善的作用也很明显，从一定意义上说，小浪底水利枢纽工程就是一个绿色、环保、生态、民生工程。小浪底水利枢

IV. Water Conservancy Projects Are Ultimately Ecological Projects

The Yellow River Basin has little water and much sand, and most of it belongs to arid and semi-arid areas, with an average annual precipitation of over 400mm. From 1919 to 1975, the average annual natural runoff of the Yellow River was 58 billion cubic meters. Since the 1990s, with the rapid growth of population and inappropriate human activities in the Yellow River Basin, the river has been breaking down year after year, with serious shrinkage of the river channel downstream and a sharp decline in flooding capacity. The self-purification capacity of the water flows has declined, water bodies are seriously polluted, and the ecological environment of the basin is under increasing pressure.

The fundamental purpose of designing and building water conservancy projects is to make comprehensive use of water resources, turning harm into benefit, which is fundamentally ecological engineering. We need to expand our engineering objectives, to increase the conservation, protection and rational allocation of water resources, not only pay attention to the economic benefits, but also to the ecological benefits, and always let the water conservancy project play an ecological function, so that it can better adapt to the needs of modern society. Some people believe that hydropower is a clean and cheap energy source and should be exploited to the maximum extent possible, and that river water should not be allowed to run off in vain. In fact, hydropower development can hardly be described as "clean" due to the unrecoverable damage it causes to the native ecosystem and water environment. Furthermore, water does not flow in the river for nothing, it is a form of ecological resource, and when it is used solely for economic gain, there will be over-exploitation and inefficient use of water resources, thus destroying the reasonable stock of resources that sustains the life of the river and the ecosystem, which will eventually be retaliated and punished by nature.

The Yellow River, the mother river of the Chinese nation, has been plagued by disasters for thousands of years. Since the founding of the PRC, the great Yellow River management practice has brought her a new lease of life. In

刘家峡（王伟摄）

纽工程与三门峡、陆浑、故县水库联合运用，并利用东平湖分洪，使黄河下游防洪标准在一定时期内基本达到千年一遇。通过小浪底水库的科学调度，实现了黄河下游连续多年不断流，对于改善生态具有非常重要的意义。小浪底水利枢纽工程的投入使用，成为"生态治黄"理念得以实现的关键所在。小浪底水库，就像一个大"水盆"，既可以拦蓄上游洪水，又可以利用水库蓄水、人工制造洪峰，减轻水库淤积，冲刷下游河道，黄河的健康生命得到有力维护，有效改善了小浪底库区和下游地区的生态环境。小浪底水库运用后，对下游河段的城市生活和工业的供

particular, the completion and use of the Xiaolangdi Water Conservancy Project has brought about important ecological benefits. In addition to the goals of flood control and silt reduction, Xiaolangdi also takes into account the comprehensive objectives of power generation and downstream water supply and irrigation, while improving the irrigation water guarantee for 40 million *mu* of arable land downstream and providing strong support for urban and rural production, living and ecological water use along the Yellow River. The most direct evidence of the improvement in the ecological environment is the fact that Henan and Shandong have been able to have a good harvest even in years of severe drought. The reservoir's role in improving the environment in the reservoir area is also obvious. In a sense, the Xiaolangdi Water Conservancy Project is a green, environmental, ecological and livelihood project. The combined operation of the Xiaolangdi Water Conservancy Project with the Sanmenxia, Luhun and Guxian reservoirs and the use of Dongping Lake to divert flood waters have enabled the lower reaches of the Yellow River to basically reach the 1,000-year flood control standard for a certain period. Through the scientific dispatching of the Xiaolangdi Reservoir, the lower reaches of the Yellow River have been continuously flowing for many years, which is of great importance for improving the ecology. The Xiaolangdi Project has become the key to the realization of the concept of "ecological management of the Yellow River". The Xiaolangdi Reservoir, like a large "Water Basin", can not only store upstream flood water, but also use the reservoir to store water, artificially create flood peaks, reduce reservoir siltation and wash downstream rivers, so that the healthy life of the Yellow River can be strongly maintained, effectively improving the ecological environment of the Xiaolangdi reservoir area and downstream areas. After it was put into use, the Xiaolangdi Reservoir has played an important role in supplying water for urban life and industry in the downstream section of the river, urban water for Tianjin, replenishing the reservoirs of Baiyangdian and Dalangdian in Hebei, ensuring the minimum ecological flow at the Lijin section, and providing water for fish breeding in the sea entrance section of the river. Since the impoundment of Xiaolangdi, the sediment deposition in the reservoir area has formed a reservoir of clear water, and the water discharged for power generation is also clear, with very little sand content. The results of the comprehensive evaluation of the reservoir's

黄河口湿地丹顶鹤

水、天津市的城市用水、河北白洋淀和大浪淀水库补水、保证利津断面的最小生态流量、向海口河段的鱼类提供繁衍用水等方面的作用巨大。自小浪底蓄水后库区泥沙沉积形成了一库清水,发电下泄水量也是清水,含沙量很小。水库水质污染程度综合评价结果表明:小浪底库区水质整体改善并趋于稳定,能够满足其功能规划Ⅲ类水质标准的要求。小浪底大坝脚下的小浪底大坝湿地公园,面积约10平方千米,各类草木上千种,水鸟175种,有天鹅、白鹭、鸳鸯、黑鹳、白鹳等珍稀禽类在此栖息,坝后保护区处处景色宜人。

water quality pollution level show that the overall water quality in the Xiaolangdi reservoir area has improved and stabilized, and can meet the requirements of its functional planning Class III water quality standards. At the foot of the Xiaolangdi Dam is the Xiaolangdi Dam Wetland Park, covering an area of about 10 square kilometers, with thousands of different kinds of grasses and trees, 175 species of water birds, with rare birds such as swans, egrets, mandarin ducks, black storks and white storks inhabiting the area, and pleasant scenery can be seen everywhere in the reserve behind the dam.

五、建立生态环境良好的黄河流域水利工程体系

从水利的角度来讲,中国是一个水资源短缺、水旱灾害频发的国家,而且水资源时间和空间分布不均。随着经济社会的快速发展和人口的不断增加,中国水资源的供需矛盾发生了根本性变化。洪涝和干旱对中国的粮食、饮水等安全问题造成了较大危害,而中国气候和地理的特点,决定了仅仅依靠河流自然调蓄不可能有效解决问题。要实现水资源优化配置,必须建设水库大坝和跨流域调水工程。

在修水库、建大坝,进行水电开发的过程中会出现一些生态问题,主要包括两个方面:一是移民问题,二是流域生态问题。首先,移民问题其实是社会管理问题,是工作问题。中国过去出现大量的水库移民遗留问题,主要是由于国家贫困,赔偿标准过低和安置不善等造成的。在总结这些问题后,近 20 多年来国家通过对开发性移民采取后期扶持,使不少老移民得到妥善安置。国务院出台的《大中型水利水电工程建设征地补偿和移民安置条例》,地方各级政府和相关机构通过加强政府管理与社会管理,切实履行好自身职责,让移民本身和间接受影响的农民都能受益,妥善做好移民工作,减少社会矛盾。其次,流域生态问题。近年来,水利水电行业高度重视生态问题,在水利工程建设的勘察、设计、施工、运行、管理等各阶段贯彻保护生态的理念,开发与保护并举,充分发挥大坝的生态功能,已经取得了很好的成效。例如:小浪底工程对保护黄河中下游生态发挥了很好的作用,黄河已经实现了从 1999 年以来 23 年不断流。同时,河口湿地也得到了很好的保护,经过这些年调水调沙河床也下切了 1.2 至 2.0 米。

在涉水工程附近区域,选择环境相对安静、水质符合规定、流速 ≤0.05m/s 的水域,通过非连续性种植分布范围广、适应能力强的苦草、菹草、轮叶黑藻和狐尾藻等沉水植物,逐步修复被破坏的水生植物生态

V. Establishing an Ecologically Sound Water Conservancy Project System in the Yellow River Basin

From the perspective of water conservation, China is a country with shortage of water resources, frequent flood and drought disasters, and uneven distribution of water resources in time and space. With rapid economic and social development and a growing population, the conflict between supply and demand for water resources in China has undergone fundamental changes. Floods and droughts have caused greater harm to the safety of food and drinking water in China, while the characteristics of our climate and geography dictate that relying solely on the natural storage of rivers is unlikely to solve the problem effectively. To achieve optimal allocation of water resources, reservoir dams and inter-basin water transfer projects must be built.

In the process of building reservoirs and dams and carrying out hydropower development several ecological problems can arise. There are two main aspects: one is the issue of migration, and the other is the ecological problems of the basin. Firstly, the migration problem is actually a social management problem and a work problem. A large number of legacy problems of reservoir migration emerged in China in the past, which were mainly due to national poverty, low compensation standards and poor resettlement. After summing up these problems, the State has taken late support through developmental migration in the past 20 years or so, so that many old migrants have been properly resettled. The State Council has issued the Regulations on Compensation for Land Expropriation and Resettlement of Migrants for the Construction of Large and Medium-Sized Water Conservancy and Hydropower Projects, and local governments at all levels and relevant agencies have been able to properly perform their duties by strengthening government and social management, so that both the migrants themselves and the farmers affected in between can benefit, properly working with migrants and reducing social conflicts. Secondly, there is the issue of watershed ecology. In recent years, the water conservancy and hydropower industry has attached great importance to ecological issues, implementing the concept of ecological protection at all stages of water conservancy project construction, including survey, design, construction,

群落，为鱼类提供良好的栖息、觅食、产卵的场所。同时，增加人工浮动鱼巢，为产黏性卵鱼类提供可靠繁育场所，以弥补水利工程对鱼类产卵场特别是产黏性卵鱼类产卵场的影响。这说明，我们越来越重视生态问题，从而建立起了生态环境良好的黄河流域水利工程体系。

以前我们修水库、建大坝的目标是开发、利用和管理水资源。如今我们修水库、建大坝的功能则需要扩展，要更加注重节约、保护和合理配置水资源。水利工程说到底是生态工程，因此我们要建立生态环境良好的黄河流域水利工程体系。

在今后的水利工程建设中，要认真考虑发挥水利工程的生态功能，对已建工程要在调度上注意生态问题，充分认识到水利枢纽工程除了防洪、灌溉、供水、发电、通航、旅游等功能以外，还应该强调一个重要的功能——保护生态，把水利工程建设成为生态环境良好的工程。

黄河水利工程对局部而言，能够减少污染物的排放，从而改善空气质量，改善局部小气候和生态环境，改善水生环境和促进渔业发展。许多水库都已成为著名的风景区，通过合理的景观设计和重建，具有广阔

绿廊 洛阳黄河湿地清水湾
Green Corridor Luoyang Yellow River Wetland Clearwater Bay

operation and management, and giving full play to the ecological functions of dams, and has achieved good results. For example, the Xiaolangdi Project has played a good role in protecting the ecology of the middle and lower reaches of the Yellow River, which has achieved 23 years of non-stop flow since 1999. At the same time, the estuarine wetlands have also been well protected, and the riverbed has been cut down by 1.2 to 2.0 meters after water and sand transfer over the years.

In the area near the water-related projects, we should select waters with relatively quiet environment, with water quality in accordance with regulations and flow velocity less than 0.05m/s, through discontinuous planting of submerged plants such as tape grass, water caltrop, hydrilla verticillata, and myriophyllum with wide distribution and strong adaptability, we will gradually repair the damaged aquatic plant ecological communities to provide good habitat, feeding and spawning places for fish. At the same time, artificial floating fish nests were added to provide reliable breeding sites for fish laying adhesive eggs to compensate for the impact of water conservancy projects on fish spawning grounds, especially for fish laying adhesive eggs spawning grounds. This shows that China is paying more and more attention to ecological issues, thus establishing an ecologically sound water conservancy engineering system in the Yellow River Basin.

In the past, China built reservoirs and dams with the goal of developing, utilizing and managing water resources. Now China needs to expand the function of reservoirs, dams, to pay more attention to the conservation, protection and rational allocation of water resources. In the end, hydraulic engineering is ecological engineering, so China needs to establish a good ecological environment of the Yellow River Basin water conservancy system.

In the future construction of water conservancy projects, serious consideration should be given to the ecological function of water conservancy projects. For the built projects, attention should be paid to ecological issues with full understanding that the protection of the ecology is an important function of water conservancy hub projects, in addition to flood control, irrigation, water supply, power generation, navigation, tourism and other functions to make the water conservancy projects environmentally ecological.

Locally, the Yellow River water conservancy projects can reduce pollutant

水面的水库成为非常美丽的公园和鸟类栖息地,极大地促进了旅游业的发展。

生态兴则文明兴,生态衰则文明衰。我们必须高度重视水利发展中的生态环境问题,用"人与自然和谐共生"的理念来正确认识并妥善处理水利工程对生态环境影响的问题,确保水利事业健康快速发展。

emissions, thus improving air quality, improving local microclimate and ecology, improving aquatic environment and promoting fishery development. Many reservoirs have become famous scenic spots, and through rational landscape design and reconstruction, reservoirs with vast water surfaces have become very beautiful parks and bird habitats, greatly contributing to tourism.

Ecological prosperity is the rise of civilization, while ecological decline is the decline of civilization. We must pay great attention to the ecological environment in the development of water conservancy, with the concept of "Harmony between Man and Nature" to correctly understand and properly deal with the ecological impact of water conservancy projects, to ensure the healthy and rapid development of water conservancy.

第四章

黄河生态文明

Chapter 4

The Yellow River Ecological Civilization

一、生态文明思想概述

梳理中国传统生态文化中蕴含的智慧、近现代以来的生态文明建设理论和习近平生态文明思想，为中国特色社会主义生态文明建设思想奠定了理论基础，对中国推进黄河流域生态文明建设，具有重要的理论意义和现实意义。

黄河是中华民族的母亲河，是中华文明最主要的发祥地，保护黄河是事关中华民族伟大复兴和永续发展的千秋大计。有史以来，黄河一直体弱多病，水患频繁，当前仍存在一些突出困难和问题。这些问题的表象在黄河，根子在流域，不仅有先天不足的客观因素制约，而且有后天失养的人为因素影响。因此，推动黄河流域生态保护和高质量发展，是中国区域协调发展和生态文明建设的重大战略问题。

河源之水（陈维达摄）

1. 中国传统生态文化

2018年5月18日至19日习近平总书记在全国生态环境保护大会

I. Overview of Ecological Civilization Thought

The wisdom contained in traditional Chinese ecological culture, theories of ecological civilization construction since the modern times and Xi Jinping's thoughts on ecological civilization have laid the theoretical foundation for the idea of ecological civilization construction of socialism with Chinese characteristics, which has important theoretical and practical significance for China to promote the construction of ecological civilization in the Yellow River Basin.

The Yellow River is the mother river of the Chinese nation and the most important source of the Chinese civilization. Thus the protection of the Yellow River is critical to the great rejuvenation and sustainable development of the Chinese nation. Throughout the history, the Yellow River has been frequently flooded. It is still causing problems now. These problems appear in the Yellow River, but the cause lies in the basin, not only because of the objective factors of congenital deficiency constraints, but also due to the human factors of lack of management. Therefore, to promote the ecological protection and high-quality development of the Yellow River Basin, is a major issue in the coordinated development of China's regional and ecological civilization construction.

1. Traditional Chinese Ecological Culture

On May 18 and 19, 2018, General Secretary Xi Jinping delivered an important speech at the National Conference on Ecological Environmental Protection. He pointed out that "The construction of ecological civilization is a fundamental plan for the sustainable development of the Chinese nation. The Chinese nation has always respected and loved nature, and the Chinese civilization stretching for more than 5,000 years has nurtured a rich ecological culture."[1] Chinese excellent traditional culture has a long and profound history,

---

[1] General Secretary Xi Jinping stresses at the National Conference on Ecological Environmental Protection Resolutely fight the battle of pollution prevention and control Promote the construction of ecological civilization to a new level[N]. People's Daily, 2018-5-20(01).

上发表重要讲话。他指出:"生态文明建设是关乎中华民族永续发展的根本大计。中华民族向来尊重自然、热爱自然,绵延 5000 多年的中华文明孕育着丰富的生态文化。"[1]中华优秀传统文化源远流长、博大精深,其中蕴含着丰富深厚的传统生态文化思想,体现了生态环境建设和保护的思想智慧。建设生态文明,需要从中华优秀传统文化中汲取智慧,在尊重自然、顺应自然、保护自然中实现人与自然和谐共生。

(1)"天人合一"

天人关系是中国古代哲学的根本观念和重要命题之一。中国传统文化中强调整体的和谐统一,而人与自然的和谐则是其中的重要组成部分。

孟子(约公元前 372 年—公元前 289 年),中国古代著名哲学家、思想家、教育家,战国时期儒家代表人物

Mencius (c. 372 BC – 289 BC), Chinese ancient famous philosopher, thinker and educator, representative of Confucianism during the Warring States period

《周易》云:"夫'大人'者,与天地合其德,与日月合其明,与四时合其序,与鬼神合其吉凶,先天而天弗违,后天而奉天时。"[2]

---

[1] 习近平总书记在全国生态环境保护大会上强调 坚决打好污染防治攻坚战 推动生态文明建设迈向新台阶[N].人民日报,2018-05-20(01).

[2] 刘彬.《易经》校释译论[M].济南:山东人民出版社,2019:33.

which contains rich and profound traditional ecological culture ideas, reflecting the wisdom of ecological environment construction and protection. To build ecological civilization, it is necessary to draw wisdom from the excellent Chinese traditional culture, and to achieve the harmonious coexistence of man and nature in respecting nature, conforming to nature and protecting nature.

(1) "The Unity of Man and Nature"

The relationship between man and nature is one of the fundamental concepts and important propositions of ancient Chinese philosophy. The harmony and unity of the whole is emphasized in traditional Chinese culture, and the harmony between man and nature is an important part of it.

The Book of Changes says: "The great man has the virtue vast as heaven and earth and the wisdom brilliant as the sun and the moon. He works in the good order as alteration of seasons and reveals good fortune and disaster in his divination miraculously as ghosts and spirits do. He takes action before heaven shows any sign and heaven never indicates the opposite. He deals with different affairs after heaven shows the signs and still he can follow the way of heaven."[1] This is a preliminary discussion of the idea of "the Unity of Man and Nature" from the moral level, meaning that nature has high morality, so man should learn from it to comply with the laws of nature. So, how to do it? Mencius gave the answer: "He who has given full play to his heart gets his nature. If he knows his nature, then he obtains his fortune. To preserve his heart and nurture his nature is to make his fortune."[2] He emphasized the consistency between humanity and natural law, and advocated that people learn from god and nature by reflecting on themselves and realizing their nature.

The ancient Chinese philosophers put forward to the idea of "Unity of human and Nature", which advocates that man and nature are one in harmony. The idea refers to not only the unity of man and nature that the universe and people both make a whole, but also the similarity of man and nature that people should

---

[1] Liu Bin. Proofreading, Interpreting and Discussing The Book of Changes [M]. Jinan: Shandong People's Publishing House, 2019:33.

[2] Mencius. Mencius [M]. Reviewed by WU Tianming and CHENG Jisong. Wuhan: Chongwen Book Bureau, 2012:249.

这是从道德层面对"天人合一"思想作出的初步论述,意思是天有高尚的道德,所以人要向天学习,去"合其德"。那么,怎样去做呢?孟子给出了答案:"尽其心者,知其性也。知其性,则知天矣。存其心,养其性,所以事天也。"[1]他强调了人道与天道的一致性,提倡人们通过反省自身、觉悟本性,向天学习,向自然学习。

中国古代哲人提出的"天人合一"思想,主张人与天地为一体,人与自然相协调。"天人合一"既是天人一致,宇宙自然是大天地,人则是一个小天地,也是天人相通,即人和自然在本质上是相通的,所以一切人事都要顺应自然规律,达到人与自然的和谐。正如老子提出的"人法地,地法天,天法道,道法自然",就是表明了人与自然的一致与相通性。西汉名儒董仲舒在前人的思想基础上结合了道、法等各派学说,提出了"天人之际,合而为一"的思想,并提到"天地人,万物之本也。天生之,地养之,人成之。天生之以孝悌,地养之以衣食,人成之以礼乐,三者相为手足,合以成体,不可一无也"[2]。他同样认为天、地、人是紧密联系在一起、不可分割的,是相互影响、相互作用而合为一体的。

董仲舒《春秋繁露》
Chunqiu Fan Lu by Dong Zhongshu

---

[1] 孟子.孟子[M].吴天明,程继松,评析.武汉:崇文书局,2012:249.

[2] 董仲舒.春秋繁露[M].张世亮,钟肇鹏,周桂钿,译注.北京:中华书局,2012:193-194.

conform to the laws of nature to achieve harmony between man and nature. As Laozi said, "Man follows the laws of earth, earth follows the laws of heaven, heaven follows the laws of the Tao, and the Tao follows the laws of nature", which shows the consistency and interconnection between man and nature. Dong Zhongshu, a famous Confucian of the Western Han Dynasty, combined the doctrines of the Tao and the Law, based on the ideas of the predecessors and put forward to the idea of "Heaven and man are united as one", and mentioned that "Heaven, earth and man are the essence of all things. We are given life by heaven, raised by the earth, and nurtured by men. Heaven gives us filial piety and brotherhood, the earth feeds us with food and clothing, and men give us rituals and music. The three are interdependent, and together they form a whole, which cannot be separated." [1] He also believed that heaven, earth, and man are closely linked and inseparable, and that they interact with each other and become a whole.

(2) "Taking and Using in Moderation"

The phrase "Taking in Moderation, Using with Restraint" first appeared in China during the Spring and Autumn and Warring States periods. In *Guanzi*, it mentions that "If you take from the people and use it in a measured way, the state will be safe, even if it is small. If you take from the people in excess of their limits and use them in excess of their limits, your country will be in danger, even if it is large." In *Shenzi*, it also states that "when the sage king is at the top, he makes the people use the resources at the right time, and when he uses them in a controlled manner, the people will have no plague". However, this is mainly about the relationship between the king and the people in terms of use and extraction, and does not have any ecological significance in terms of protecting the natural environment.

Lu Zhi, a famous minister of the Middle Tang Dynasty, proposed the *Six Articles on the Equalization of Taxes and Compassion for the People*, advocating that "the use should be moderate" and that "the income should be measured to

---

[1] Dong Zhongshu. Chunqiu Fanlu [M]. Interpreted and annotated by ZHANG Shiliang, Zhong Zhaopeng and Zhou Guidian. Beijing: Zhonghua Book Company, 2012:193-194.

（2）"取用有节"

"取之有度，用之有节"的说法，在中国最早出现于春秋战国时期。《管子》云："取于民有度，用之有止，国虽小必安。取于民无度，用之不止，国虽大必危。"《慎子》中也有"圣王在上，则使人有时，而用之有节，则民无疾疢"的说法。但是，这里主要讲的是君对民的取用关系，并不具有保护自然环境的生态意义。

中唐名相陆贽上疏提出了《均节赋税恤百姓六条》，主张"用之有节""量入为出"，反对无限度地向百姓征收赋税。他还强调自然资源有限，要求"取之有度，用之有节"，反对盲目无限度地开发和利用自然资源，具有保护自然生态的内涵。

司马光在《资治通鉴》里讲："地力之生物有大数，人力之成物有大限。取之有度，用之有节，则常足；取之无度，用之无节，则常不足。"意思是说，靠自然的力量生长之物是有数的，人的力量创造之物也是有限度的。取用时有限度，使用时能节制的话，自然界的资源就常常能满足人们的需要；取用时没有限度，使用时不能节制的话，自然界的资源就不能一直满足人们的需要。

司马光《资治通鉴》
History as a Mirror by Sima Guang

2. 近现代生态文明理论

社会发展总是在一定的历史条件下进行的，这一进程一方面离不开生态环境的因素，另一方面也对生态环境产生一定的影响。

the expenditure", and opposing the imposition of unlimited taxes on the people. He also emphasized that natural resources were limited and demanded that they should be taken in moderation and used in moderation, opposing the blind and unlimited exploitation of natural resources, with the connotation of protecting the natural ecology.

Sima Guang said in *History as a Mirror*: "There is a great number of creatures in the earth, and a great limit to what can be made by human power. If you take in measure and use in moderation, you will always have enough; if you take without measure and use without moderation, you will always have not enough." This means that there is a limit to the number of things that can be grown by the power of nature, and there is a limit to the number of things that can be created by the power of man. If there is a limit to what can be taken and if it can be used with restraint, the resources of nature will always be sufficient to meet people's needs; if there is no limit to what can be taken and if it cannot be used with restraint, the resources of nature will not always meet people's needs.

2. Modern Ecological Civilization Theory

Social development has always taken place under certain historical conditions, a process that on the one hand cannot be separated from ecological factors and on the other hand has a certain impact on the ecological environment.

(1) Ecological and Environmental Problems in the Modern Times

In modern times, Western countries such as Britain and France brought with them advanced scientific and technological means and modern industrial production methods when they invaded China, and then China was gradually reduced to a semi-colonial and semi-feudal society. This drastic upheaval brought about huge changes to the entire social and ecological environment, and the natural ecological environment was more seriously damaged, thus triggering a series of ecological crises and greatly affecting people's lives.

Overall, the development of modern industry, a chaotic and unsettling social environment and the plundering of China's rich natural resources by imperialism led to frequent ecological and environmental problems. In this context, the rapid development of industry in modern China led to changes in the natural ecology, and industrial civilization focused on the relationship between man and man, thus

（1）近代以来的生态环境问题

近代以来，英国、法国等西方国家在入侵中国的同时带来了先进的科学技术手段和现代化的工业生产方式，在这个过程中，中国逐渐沦为半殖民地半封建社会。这种急剧动荡给整个社会生态环境带来了巨大的变化，自然生态环境遭到了较为严重的破坏，从而引发了一系列生态危机，人民生活也受到了极大影响。

总体来看，近代工业的发展、混乱不安的社会环境和帝国主义对中国丰富自然资源的掠夺导致了频发的生态环境问题。在这种情况下，近代中国工业的迅速发展导致自然生态发生变化，工业文明重在处理人与人之间的关系，从而忽视了作为人类生存和发展基础的生态环境问题，导致了人与自然之间的关系失衡，最终产生了人类的生存与发展危机。此时，整个中国社会的生态文明程度是不高的。

（2）新中国成立以来的生态文明理论

新中国成立以来，历届党的领导集体在进行经济、政治、文化建设的过程中，一直高度关注人与自然的关系问题，在继承马克思恩格斯生态思想的基础上，结合中国的具体实际，形成了一系列生态文明建设的思想理论成果，这对于我们谋求生态优先、绿色发展以及实现人与自然和谐相处具有重要的指导意义。

以毛泽东同志为核心的党的第一代领导集体立足国情，对中国社会主义生态文明建设事业进行探索，虽然没有提出明确的生态文明建设的理论，但从马克思主义认识论的角度出发，提出了植树造林、绿化祖国，兴修水利、治理水患，制定环境保护法规等一系列有利于环境保护的措施。

（3）改革开放以来的生态文明理论

以邓小平同志为核心的党的第二代领导集体把环境保护确定为一项基本国策，制定了中国环境保护事业的战略方针与相关法治建设政策，强调要在资源开发利用中通过依靠科学技术来解决生态环境问题，重视

neglecting the ecological and environmental issues that underpin human survival and development, leading to an imbalance in the relationship between man and nature, which ultimately produced a crisis of human survival and development. At this time, the degree of ecological civilization in Chinese society as a whole was not high.

(2) Theories of Ecological Civilization since the Founding of New China

Since the founding of New China, the successive CPC leaders have been highly concerned with the relationship between man and nature in the process of economic, political and cultural construction, and have formed a series of ideological and theoretical achievements in the construction of ecological civilization based on the inheritance of ecological thoughts of Marx and Engels and the specific reality of China. This is of great significance to our pursuit of ecological priority and green development, as well as the achievement of harmony between man and nature.

The first generation of the CPC leadership, with Comrade Mao Zedong at its core, explored the cause of building a socialist ecological civilization in China based on national conditions. Although it did not put forward a clear theory of building an ecological civilization, it proposed a series of measures conducive to environmental protection from the perspective of Marxist epistemology, such as planting trees and greening the motherland; constructing water conservancy and combating floods; and enacting environmental protection regulations.

(3) Theories of Ecological Civilization since the Reform and Opening up

The second generation of the CPC leadership, with Comrade Deng Xiaoping at its core, established environmental protection as a basic state policy; formulated strategic guidelines for China's environmental protection and related rule of law; and emphasized the need to solve ecological and environmental problems through reliance on science and technology in the exploitation of resources and the importance of ecological and environmental protection.

The third generation of the CPC's central leadership, with Comrade Jiang Zemin at its core, emphasized the need to harmonize economic development with environmental protection, and established sustainable development as China's national strategy. It also put forward the scientific assertion that "to protect the ecological environment is to protect the productive forces" and, from a global

生态环境保护。

以江泽民同志为核心的党的第三代中央领导集体强调要将经济发展与环境保护相统一，把可持续发展确定为治国方略，阐明了"保护生态环境就是保护生产力"的科学论断，并站在全球化的视角提出要借鉴国外环境保护的先进技术与经验，从而不断推进国内生态环境建设。

以胡锦涛同志为总书记的党中央提出了科学发展观这一重大战略思想，为中国特色社会主义生态文明建设思想奠定了理论基础；特别强调要统筹人与自然和谐发展，要牢固树立生态文明观念；指明了调整经济结构和转变经济增长方式应成为中国生态文明建设的着力点；提出了构建资源节约型与环境友好型社会的先进理念。

perspective, proposed to draw on the advanced technology and experience of foreign countries in environmental protection, so as to continuously promote the construction of the domestic ecological environment.

The CPC with Comrade Hu Jintao as its General Secretary, put forward the major strategic idea of the scientific outlook on development, laying the theoretical foundation for the idea of building a socialist ecological civilization with Chinese characteristics; particularly emphasizing the need to co-ordinate the harmonious development of man and nature and to firmly establish the concept of ecological civilization; indicating that adjusting the economic structure and transforming the mode of economic growth should become the focus of China's ecological civilization; and putting forward the advanced concept of building a resource-saving and environment-friendly society.

二、习近平生态文明思想

在浙江工作期间,习近平同志对生态文明建设作了多方面重要论述,强调发展理念、发展方式的深刻转变,揭示了现代化进程中生态文明建设规律。党的十八大首次明确提出"五位一体"的中国特色社会主义总体布局,生态文明建设上升成为党的执政方针。站在中国特色社会主义事业全面发展和实现"中国梦"的战略高度,习近平总书记提出了"人与自然和谐共生""人与自然生命共同体""绿水青山就是金山银山"等新论断,逐步形成了习近平生态文明思想。

1."人与自然和谐共生"思想

"人与自然和谐共生"思想是习近平生态文明思想的重要内容。习近平总书记在从哲学思维角度把握中华传统生态思想的基础上,提出了"人与自然和谐共生"理念,以整体、综合的思维去认识和处理人与自然的关系。2017年10月18日,习近平总书记在党的十九大报告中,把"坚持人与自然和谐共生"作为新时代坚持和发展中国特色社会主义的基本方略之一进行了重要论述。党的十九届五中全会进一步对"推动绿色发展,促进人与自然和谐共生"做出战略安排。2021年4月30日在十九届中央政治局第二十九次集体学习时,习近平总书记强调,要完整、准确、全面贯彻新发展理念,保持战略定力,站在人与自然和谐共生的高度来谋划经济社会发展,努力建设人与自然和谐共生的现代化。

马克思、恩格斯指出:"人是自然界的一部分,人的肉体生活和精神生活同自然界相联系。"[1]在此理论观点的基础上,习近平总书记结合中国具体生态实践,明确指出:"人因自然而生,人与自然是一种

---

[1] 马克思,恩格斯.马克思恩格斯选集:第1卷[M].北京:人民出版社,1995:45.

Ⅱ. Xi Jinping's Ecological Civilization Thought

During his presidency in Zhejiang Province, Comrade Xi Jinping made important remarks on the construction of ecological civilization, and emphasized the profound transformation of development concepts and methods, which revealed the laws of ecological civilization construction in the process of modernization. The Party's 18th National Congress first clearly put forward the "Five-In-One" overall layout of socialism with Chinese characteristics, and the construction of ecological civilization was elevated to the Party's governing policy. Standing at the strategic height of the comprehensive development of socialism with Chinese characteristics and the realization of the "Chinese Dream", General Secretary Xi Jinping has proposed the "Harmonious Coexistence of Man and Nature", "Community of Life between Man and Nature", and "Green mountains and clear water are equal to mountains of gold and silver", gradually forming Xi Jinping's thought on ecological civilization.

1. The Idea of "Harmony and Coexistence between Man and Nature"

The idea of "Harmony and Coexistence between Man and Nature" is an important element of Xi Jinping's thought on ecological civilization. Based on the traditional Chinese ecological thought from the perspective of philosophical thinking, General Secretary Xi Jinping put forward the idea of "Harmony and Coexistence between Man and Nature" with a holistic and comprehensive thinking to understand and deal with the relationship between man and nature. On October 18, 2017, in the report of the 19th National Congress of the CPC, General Secretary Xi Jinping made an important statement on "Adhering to the Harmony and Coexistence between Man and Nature" as one of the basic strategies for upholding and developing socialism with Chinese characteristics in the new era. And strategic arrangements were then made for "promoting green development and preserving harmonious coexistence between man and nature" on the Fifth Plenary Session of the 19th CPC Central Committee. On April 30, 2021, during the 29th collective study of the Political Bureau of the CPC Central Committee, General Secretary Xi Jinping stressed that the new development

共生的关系。"[1]首先，生态环境破坏已成为最突出的民生问题之一，它不仅威胁到人们的身体健康和生命安全，还会影响到人们的生存空间和社会发展。因此，习近平总书记提出："要像保护眼睛一样保护生态环境，像对待生命一样对待生态环境，让中华大地天更蓝、山更绿、水更清、环境更优美。"[2]同时，习近平总书记又提出了一系列生态文明建设的指导意见，如：建立生态环境保护制度、树立生态环境保护意识等。其次，自然生态环境问题制约中国经济发展和社会进步。他在浙江明确指出："你善待环境，环境是友好的；你污染环境，环境总有一天会翻脸，会毫不留情地报复你。"[3]因此，改善生态环境就是造福人类。最后，人类社会历史发展的经验表明，一个国家或民族能否一直蓬勃发展就在于人们赖以生存的生态环境是否得到维持，生态环境的状态是影响人类文明兴衰的重要因素。因此，我们更要处理好人类社会发展和自然生态环境的关系。

2. "人与自然生命共同体"思想

党的十八大以来，习近平总书记提出了人与自然构成"生命共同体"的思想。他指出："山水林田湖是一个生命共同体，人的命脉在田，田的命脉在水，水的命脉在山，山的命脉在土，土的命脉在树。"[4]该论述清晰地揭示了生态环境在人类生存和发展过程中的基础性地位，强调了山水林田湖草沙是生命共同体，推进生态文明建设，需要符合生态的系统性，坚持系统思维、协同推进。只有尊重人类生态环境的系统性和规律性，才能实现人类与自然生态环境的和谐，反之则会遭到自然生

---

[1] 习近平.习近平谈治国理政：第2卷[M].北京：外文出版社，2017:394.

[2] 习近平.习近平谈治国理政：第2卷[M].北京：外文出版社，2017:395.

[3] 习近平.之江新语[M].杭州：浙江人民出版社，2007:11.

[4] 习近平.十八大以来重要文献选编（上）[M].北京：中央文献出版社，2014:507.

concept should be implemented completely, accurately and comprehensively, and socioeconomic development should be planned from the perspective of the harmony and coexistence of man and nature so as to build the modernization with harmony between man and nature.

Marx and Engels stated that "Man is a part of nature and his physical and spiritual life is connected with nature."[1] General Secretary Xi Jinping, taking into account China's specific ecological practices, clearly pointed out that "man is born out of nature, and man and nature are in a symbiotic relationship."[2] Firstly, ecological and environmental damage has become one of the most prominent livelihood issues, which not only threatens people's health and life safety, but also affects their living space and social development. Therefore, General Secretary Xi Jinping proposed, "We should protect the ecological environment as if it were our eyes, and treat it as if it were our lives, so that the Chinese land will have a bluer sky, greener mountains, clearer water and a more beautiful environment."[3] At the same time, General Secretary Xi Jinping put forward a series of guidelines for the construction of ecological civilization, such as establishing an ecological environmental protection system and building awareness of ecological environmental protection. Secondly, natural ecological and environmental problems constrain our economic development and social progress. He clearly pointed out in Zhejiang province: "If you treat the environment well, the environment is friendly; if you pollute the environment, the environment will turn against you one day and will retaliate against you without mercy."[4] Therefore, to improve the ecological environment is to benefit mankind. Finally, the experience of the historical development of human society shows that

---

[1] Marx, Engels. Selected Works of Marx and Engels (Vol. 1) [M]. Beijing: People's Publishing House, 1995:45.

[2] Xi Jinping. The Governance of China (Vol. 2) [M]. Beijing: Foreign Languages Press, 2017:394.

[3] Xi Jinping. The Governance of China (Vol. 2) [M]. Beijing: Foreign Languages Press, 2017:395.

[4] Xi Jinping. Zhijiang Xinyu [M]. Hangzhou: Zhejiang People's Publishing House, 2007:11.

态环境的报复,最终给人类生存和发展带来危害。

习近平总书记在党的十九大报告中指出:"人与自然是生命共同体,人类必须尊重自然、顺应自然、保护自然。"人因自然而生,改变自然、征服自然、破坏自然最终只会伤及人类自身,尊重自然、顺应自然、保护自然才是人类唯一的正确选择。首先,要"尊重自然"。面对生命之源的自然,人类应常怀敬畏之心,对大自然的开发利用要以尊重自然规律为前提。正如习近平总书记所言:"你善待环境,环境是友好的;你污染环境,环境总有一天会翻脸,会毫不留情地报复你。"[1]其次,要"顺应自然"。人们在利用自然、改造自然以满足自身需要时要把握和遵循自然规律。只有顺应自然规律,才能更好地实现人类进步和社会发展。最后,要"保护自然"。保护自然生态环境就是保护人类自己。习近平总书记指出:"我们要坚持节约资源和保护环境的基本国策,像保护眼睛一样保护生态环境,像对待生命一样对待生态。"[2]因此,我们要遵循自然规律、顺应自然,才能真正做到尊重自然,最终达到保护自然的目的。

随着世界经济的全球化、一体化发展,国际社会日益成为密切联系、相互作用的统一整体,对于生态危机的治理就成了客观必然的全球性问题。面对全球性的生态危机,习近平总书记提出了"命运共同体"这一人类社会的新理念:"到目前为止,地球是人类唯一赖以生存的家园,珍爱和呵护地球是人类唯一的选择。中国的方案是:构建人类命运共同体,实现共赢共享。"[3]这一理念展现了中国对全球生态危机治理的大国担当,对推动世界各国共同承担全球生态危机治理责任和实现全球生态危机治理合作交流具有重要的意义。"人类命运共同体"思想不仅

---

[1] 习近平.之江新语[M].杭州:浙江人民出版社,2017:141.

[2] 习近平.习近平谈治国理政:第2卷[M].北京:外文出版社,2017:209.

[3] 习近平.习近平谈治国理政:第2卷[M].北京:外文出版社,2017:538-539.

whether a country or nation can always flourish depends on the maintenance of the ecological environment on which people depend, and the state of the ecological environment is an important factor affecting the rise and fall of human civilization. It is therefore all the more important that we manage the relationship between human social development and the natural ecological environment.

2. The Idea of "Community of Life between Man and Nature"

Since the 18th CPC Congress, General Secretary Xi Jinping has put forward the idea that human and nature constitute a "Community of Life", pointing out that "mountains, water, forests, fields and lakes are a community of life. The lifeblood of human is in the fields, the lifeblood of the fields is in the water, the lifeblood of the water is in the mountains, the lifeblood of the mountains is in the soil, and the lifeblood of the soil is in the trees."[1] It clearly reveals the fundamental position of the ecological environment in the process of human survival and development, emphasizing that the mountains, water, forests, fields, lakes, grasses and sand are a community of life, and to promote the construction of ecological civilization, it is necessary to conform to the systemic nature of ecology, adhere to the systemic thinking and synergy. Only by respecting the systemic and regular nature of human ecological environment can we achieve harmony between human beings and natural ecological environment, or vice versa, we will be retaliated by natural ecological environment and eventually bring harm to human survival and development.

General Secretary Xi Jinping pointed out in the report of the 19th CPC Congress that "human and nature are a community of life, and mankind must respect nature, conform to nature, and protect nature." Human is born of nature, changing nature, conquering nature and destroying nature will only hurt mankind itself in the end, respecting nature, conforming to nature and protecting nature is the only correct choice for mankind. First of all, we must "respect nature". In the face of nature, the source of life, humans should always be in awe of nature, the exploitation of nature to respect the laws of nature as a prerequisite. As General

---

[1] Xi Jinping. *Selected Important Documents Since the 18th National Congress (I)* [M]. Beijing: Central Literature Publishing House, 2014:507.

第四章 黄河生态文明

四川省若尔盖（董保华摄）

丰富和发展了生态文明思想，同时也为实现中华民族伟大复兴创造了良好的生态空间。

Secretary Xi Jinping said, "If you treat the environment well, the environment is friendly; if you pollute the environment, the environment will one day turn against you and will retaliate without mercy." [1] Secondly, we should "follow nature". People must understand and follow the laws of nature when making use of and transforming the nature to meet our own demands. Only by following the laws of nature can we better achieve human progress and social development. Finally, to "protect nature". To protect the natural ecological environment is to protect human beings themselves. General Secretary Xi Jinping pointed out that "we must adhere to the basic state policy of conserving resources and protecting the environment, protecting the ecological environment like an eye, and treating the ecology as life." [2] Therefore, we have to follow the laws of nature and conform to nature in order to truly respect nature and ultimately achieve the purpose of protecting nature.

With the globalization and integration of the world economy, the international community is becoming a unified whole with close ties and interactions, and the management of ecological crises has become an objective and inevitable global issue. In the face of the global ecological crisis, General Secretary Xi Jinping proposed a new concept of "Community of Human Destiny" for human society: "So far, the Earth is the only home for human beings to survive, and cherishing and caring for the Earth is the only choice for human beings. China's solution is to build a community of human destiny and achieve win-win sharing." [3] This concept shows China's responsible role as a great power in taking the initiative for global ecological crisis management, and is of great significance in promoting countries around the world to jointly assume responsibility for global ecological crisis management and achieving cooperation and exchange in global ecological crisis management. The idea of "Community

---

[1] Xi Jinping. Zhijiang Xinyu [M]. Hangzhou: Zhejiang People's Publishing House, 2017:141.

[2] Xi Jinping. The Governance of China (Vol. 2) [M]. Beijing: Foreign Languages Press, 2017:209.

[3] Xi Jinping. The Governance of China (Vol. 2) [M]. Beijing: Foreign Languages Press, 2017:538-539.

3."绿水青山就是金山银山"思想

2005年8月15日,时任浙江省委书记的习近平同志在浙江湖州安吉考察时,首次提出了"绿水青山就是金山银山"的科学论断。此后,他进一步阐述了"两山"论述中的三个阶段问题。在担任总书记后,习近平同志仍多次强调"绿水青山就是金山银山",他提出:"我们既要绿水青山,也要金山银山。宁要绿水青山,不要金山银山,而且绿水青

青海玛多黄河乡的湿地(董保华摄)

with a shared future for mankind" not only enriches and develops the thought of ecological civilization, but also creates a good ecological space for the realization of the great rejuvenation of the Chinese nation.

3. "Green Mountains and Clear Water are Equal to Mountains of Gold and Silver"

On August 15, 2005, Comrade Xi Jinping, then Secretary of the Zhejiang Provincial Party Committee, first put forward the scientific assertion that "Green mountains and clear water are equal to mountains of gold and silver" during his inspection in Anji, Huzhou city, Zhejiang Province. Since then, he has further elaborated on the three stages of the "Two Mountains" theory. After becoming general secretary, Comrade Xi Jinping still emphasized "green mountains and clear water are equal to mountains of gold and silver" many times, and he proposed: "We want both clear water and green hills and mountains of gold and silver. Rather clear water and green mountains, not the golden mountains, and green mountains and clear water are equal to mountains of gold and silver." [1] The "Two Mountains" theory fully embodies the dialectical viewpoint of Marxism, systematically analyzes the interrelationship between economy and ecology in the evolutionary process, and deeply reveals the basic laws of economic and social development.

Since the 18th CPC Congress, the Party Central Committee, with Comrade Xi Jinping at its core, has incorporated the construction of ecological civilization into the overall layout of "Five-In-One" while insisting on economic development, and written the concept of "insisting on green mountains and clear water are equal to mountains of gold and silver" into the central document. This is a major change in the concept of socialist construction with Chinese characteristics. On October 18, 2017, General Secretary Xi Jinping pointed out in the report of the 19th National Congress that: to adhere to the harmonious coexistence of man and nature, we must establish and practice the concept of "green mountains and

---

[1] Publicity Department of the CPC Central Committee Readings from the Series of Important Speeches by General Secretary Xi Jinping [M]. Beijing: Study Publishing House, 2016:230.

山就是金山银山。"[1]"两山"理论充分体现了马克思主义的辩证观点，系统剖析了经济与生态在演进过程中的相互关系，深刻揭示了经济社会发展的基本规律。

党的十八大以来，以习近平同志为核心的党中央在坚持发展经济的同时，将生态文明建设纳入到"五位一体"的总体布局之中，并将"坚持绿水青山就是金山银山"的理念写进中央文件，实现了中国特色社会主义建设实践理念的重大转变。2017年10月18日，习近平总书记在十九大报告中指出：坚持人与自然和谐共生，必须树立和践行"绿水青山就是金山银山"的理念，坚持节约资源和保护环境的基本国策。

习近平生态文明思想继承并发展了马克思主义生态哲学思想，吸收了中国传统优秀生态文化中的智慧思想，同时也对近现代西方生态文明理论进行了批判性借鉴，不仅为中国社会主义生态文明建设提供了重要的理论指南，也进一步丰富和完善了马克思主义生态文明建设思想理论体系。

---

[1] 中共中央宣传部.习近平总书记系列重要讲话读本[M].北京：学习出版社，2016:230.

clear water are equal to mountains of gold and silver" and adhere to the basic state policy of saving resources and protecting the environment.

Xi Jinping's thought on ecological civilization inherits and develops Marxist ecological philosophy and absorbs the wisdom ideas in traditional Chinese excellent ecological culture, while also critically drawing on modern Western ecological civilization theories, which not only provides an important theoretical guide for the construction of socialist ecological civilization in China, but also further enriches and improves the theoretical system of Marxist ecological civilization construction thought.

三、黄河流域生态保护和修复

黄河是中华民族的母亲河。2019年9月18日，习近平总书记在黄河流域生态保护和高质量发展座谈会上发表重要讲话，提出要坚持绿水青山就是金山银山的理念，坚持生态优先、绿色发展，强调着力加强生态保护治理，促进全流域高质量发展，让黄河成为造福人民的幸福河。

保护黄河是事关中华民族伟大复兴的千秋大计。习近平总书记指出，黄河流域生态保护和高质量发展，同京津冀协同发展、长江经济带发展、粤港澳大湾区建设、长三角一体化发展一样，是重大国家战略。

改革开放以来，中国社会经济飞速发展，城市化进程加快，水资源面临着越来越大的压力。按照国际通行的标准，如果水资源开发利用率超过40%就会引起严重的生态环境问题。近年来，中国很多地区相继出现了相关的生态环境问题。其中，黄河流域的水生态环境压力比较大，在一定程度上也影响和制约了中国社会经济的健康发展。生态环境是人类赖以生存和发展的基础和前提，要明确水土保持在黄河流域生态保护与高质量发展中的位置。

1. 历史上的黄河流域生态保护的措施

历史上的黄河在造就中华民族灿烂文明的同时，也给中华民族带来了无尽的苦难。东西方历史中有关洪荒时代和挪亚方舟的记载便是证明。而黄河带给人们的苦难主要是决口和改道后的大洪水。决口和改道的原因，除人为之外，就是从黄河中上游带来的大量泥沙堆积，抬高河床，导致决堤和改道。因此，治河必须治沙。但是治沙对于古时候的人们来说，需要一个认识的过程。

黄河泥沙主要来自黄河中游的水土流失。现今的考古证明，早在遥远的地质历史时期，强烈的土壤侵蚀就已经把黄土高原切割成了千沟万

III. The Yellow River Basin Ecological Protection and Restoration

The Yellow River is the mother river of the Chinese nation. On September 18, 2019, General Secretary Xi Jinping delivered an important speech at the Symposium on Ecological Protection and High-quality Development of the Yellow River Basin, proposing to adhere to the concept "green mountains and clear water are equal to mountains of gold and silver", adhere to ecological priority and green development, emphasizing efforts to strengthen ecological protection and regulation, promote high-quality development of the entire basin, so that the Yellow River becomes a happy river for the benefit of the people.

The protection of the Yellow River is critical to the great rejuvenation and sustainable development of the Chinese nation. General Secretary Xi Jinping pointed out that the Yellow River Basin Ecological Protection and High-quality Development, along with Beijing-Tianjin-Hebei synergistic development, the development of the Yangtze River Economic Belt, the construction of Guangdong, Hong Kong and Macao Bay Area, the Yangtze River Delta integrated development, is a major national strategy.

Since the Reform and Opening up, with the rapid development of China's society and economy, the pace of urbanization has also been speeding up, for which water resources are facing increasing pressure. According to the internationally accepted standard, if the utilization rate of water resources development exceeds 40%, it will cause serious ecological and environmental problems. In recent years, related ecological and environmental problems have emerged in many areas of China one after another. Among them, the water ecological environment in the Yellow River Basin is under greater pressure, which to a certain extent also affects and restricts the healthy socio-economic development of China. Ecological environment is the basis and prerequisite for human survival and development, and it is necessary to clarify the position of soil and water conservation in the ecological protection and high-quality development

垫，而冲击到下游地区的泥沙则堆积形成了华北平原。这完全是大自然的造化，其间的功过也无从评说。进入人类历史时期以后，黄土高原的土壤侵蚀有增无减，这主要源自人们在黄河中游地区的农耕活动。黄河中下游干流的泥沙，也是从史前时期起就一直居高不下。历史文献记载表明，黄河自古就是一条充满泥沙的浑浊河流，黄河这一名称就取自它的水中饱含黄土泥沙，致使水色浑黄，因此，黄河的名称本身就带着黄土地的烙印。

于是，历史上黄河生态问题主要围绕阻止黄河的河水泛滥、河道修复、加固、还原、改道等展开。

为了治理黄河泛滥，远古时期大禹的父亲鲧采用"堤埂壅障法"治水，但成效甚微。随后，大禹通过"疏顺导滞法"治理黄河水。大禹所采用的疏导办法比他父亲鲧的壅障法显然前进了一大步，它可以照顾到更大的范围，从"障"到"疏"，这是治河方略上的第一次重要发展。但是，"疏"是在"障"的基础上发展起来的，并不等于抛弃"障"。此后，在"疏"的基础上，人们又发展了系统的河岸堤防，实现了由限洪到防洪的飞跃，从而使堤防成为主要的防洪手段，这是治河方略上的第二次重大发展。

前人发明了植树固堤的办法，到明朝时有了很大发展。明代的治水名臣刘天河总结出"植柳六法"，方法非常高超。明代在堤防技术上的最大发展是固堤放淤技术的普遍应用。[1]在北宋王安石变法期间，曾经大规模地在黄河干流上引水淤地。由于朝廷的鼓励和提倡，一时间，引黄放淤形成高潮，利用黄河泥沙淤成的田地非常肥沃，对促进沿黄地带农业生产的发展起到了重要作用。但直到明代以前，引黄放淤一直基本上限制在农田水利的范畴内，没有利用它来作为治河手段。明隆庆末年，万恭担任总理河道，负责黄河的整治工作，提出了固堤放淤的办法，取得了良好的效果。作为具体的工程措施后，在以堤防为主的前提下，

---

[1] 辛德勇.黄河史话[M].北京：社会科学文献出版社，2013：134.

of the Yellow River Basin.

1. Historical Measures for Ecological Protection of the Yellow River Basin

The Yellow River in history has brought endless suffering to the Chinese people while creating a splendid civilization. This is evidenced by the accounts of the Flood Age and Noah's Ark in Eastern and Western history. The suffering brought by the Yellow River is mainly due to the floods after the break and the diversion. The reason for the breakage and diversion, apart from man-made causes, is the accumulation of large amounts of sediment brought from the middle and upper reaches of the Yellow River, which raises the riverbed and causes the breakage and diversion. Therefore, sand control is necessary for river management. But it took a long time for people in ancient times to realize the importance of sand control.

The Yellow River sediment mainly comes from soil erosion in the middle reaches of the Yellow River. According to the present-day archaeological description, as early as in the distant geological history period, strong soil erosion had cut the Loess Plateau into thousands of ravines, and the soil scoured to the downstream area formed the North China Plain, which is entirely the creation of nature, and the merits and demerits of the period cannot be judged. After entering the period of human history, the soil erosion on the Loess Plateau has been increasing, which mainly originates from people's farming activities in the middle reaches of the Yellow River. The sediment in the middle and lower reaches of the Yellow River has also been high since prehistoric times. Historical documents show that the Yellow River is a muddy river full of sediment since ancient times, the name of the Yellow River is taken from its water full of sediment, resulting in a yellow color, therefore, the name of the Yellow River itself has all kinds of connections with the Yellow Earth.

Thus, historically, the ecological problems of the Yellow River revolved around stopping the river flooding, river restoration, reinforcement, restoration, and diversion.

In order to control the flooding of the Yellow River, in ancient times, the Father of Dayu, named Gun, used the "dike blocking method" to control the water, but with little effects. Subsequently, Dayu managed the Yellow River

往往也并用疏浚的办法，特别是在河水改道漫流时期，想要使其归入稳定的河道，更要依赖疏浚的办法。如历史文献记载中，王景治河、贾鲁治河，就是采用疏、浚、塞三者并举。

贾鲁治河
Jia Lu Regulating the River

在利用疏浚方法治河方面，宋朝人还做过一件虽然失败了但很有意义的尝试。黄河不断泛滥乃至改道，在很大程度上是泥沙在下游河床上淤积而造成堵塞，致使泄水不畅引起的。但长期以来，人们对于这种严重淤积一直束手无策。北宋神宗熙宁六年（1073年），在王安石的主持下，成立了一个专门负责疏浚河道的"疏浚黄河司"，试图采用专门的机械来清除河道中的淤泥。

当时有一个叫李公义的人发明了一种船载挖泥工具，名为"铁笼爪扬泥车"。[1]从理论上看，这种淘浚工具的设计就有严重缺陷。泥沙在黄河下游大量淤积，是河水中泥沙含量超过水流的负载而造成的。在

---

[1] 辛德勇.黄河史话[M].北京：社会科学文献出版社，2013:112.

water by "dredging and channeling". The diversion method adopted by Dayu was obviously a big step forward from his father's "blocking method", which could take care of a larger area, from "blocking" to "dredging", which was the first important development in the river management strategy. This is the first important development of the river management strategy. However, "dredging" was developed on the basis of "blocking", which was not the same as abandoning "blocking". After that, on the basis of "dredging", people developed a system of riverbank embankments, which made a leap from flood control to flood prevention, thus making embankments the main means of flood control, which was the second important development in river regulation strategy.

The previous people invented the method of planting trees to strengthen the dike, which was greatly developed in the Ming Dynasty. The famous water management expert Liu Tianhe summed up the "six methods of planting willows", which is a very advanced method. The greatest development in embankment technology during the Ming Dynasty was the widespread application of techniques for strengthening dykes and releasing silt.[1] During Wang Anshi's change of law in the Northern Song Dynasty, flood warping land was adopted in the mainstream of the Yellow River on a large scale. of the Yellow River on a large scale. Due to the encouragement and promotion of the imperial court, the siltation reached a climax, and the fields made from the siltation of the Yellow River were very fertile and played an important role in promoting the development of agricultural production along the Yellow River. But until the Ming Dynasty, the siltation of the Yellow River has been basically restricted to the scope of agricultural water conservancy, not using it as a means of river management. In the last year of Longqing, Ming Dynasty, Wang Gong, the Prime Minister of the river, who was responsible for the improvement of the Yellow River, put forward the approach of solid dikes and siltation, which achieved good results. After specific engineering measures, embankments were used as the main means, and often dredging was also used, especially during periods of diversion and diffuse flow of the river, where dredging was vital to bring the river back to a

---

[1] Xin Deyong. The History of the Yellow River [M]. Beijing: Social Science Literature Press, 2013:134.

这种情况下,如果不能提高水流的挟沙能力,即使搅起了沉淤的泥沙,它也会很快在不远的地方沉淀下来,不会对浚深河床起到任何作用,所以这一次淘浚淤积泥沙的尝试,不可避免地失败了。尽管如此,这种重视清除河床淤积的治河指导思想及勇于探索的精神却是值得充分肯定的。它在近千年前,为中国人民试图以机械力量解决黄河淤积问题开了先河。

河患不断,也产生了许多治河主张,其中最著名的是贾让的"治河三策"。贾让的上策是主张人为河流改道。当时,黄河下游河床已经淤高,有些地方在涨水时水面高出堤外民屋,成了典型的悬河。因此,人为改道的设想可以说是基于对黄河河患根本原因的认识而提出的。贾让的中策是分流河水,就是引一部分水流沿太行山冲积扇前缘地带北行,从中引渠灌溉,这样做可以分解黄河干流的水量,旱则引水灌溉,解除旱灾,洪涝时可宣泄洪水,防止溃决干流,同时分出的支流可以兼具航运的作用,这种主张作为一种治河方略,可以称为"分流派"。贾让的下策是沿袭一般的方法,加高培厚原有堤防,维持现存河道。[1]

贾让
Jia Rang

---

[1] 辛德勇.黄河史话[M].北京:社会科学文献出版社,2013:121-122.

stable course. As recorded in historical documents, Wang Jing and Jia Lu used a combination of dredging, deepening and plugging when they regulated the river.

In terms of using dredging methods to manage rivers, the Song Dynasty also made an unsuccessful but significant attempt. The constant flooding and diversion of the Yellow River was caused to a large extent by the blockage caused by the siltation of sediment in the riverbed downstream, resulting in poor water discharge. For a long time, however, there was nothing that could be done about this severe siltation. In the sixth year of the reign of Emperor Zhaoxu of the Northern Song Dynasty (1073), a "Yellow River Dredging Division" was set up under the auspices of Wang Anshi with an attempt to remove the silt from the river by means of special machinery.

At that time, a man called Li Gongyi invented a boat-mounted dredging tool called the "iron cage claw dredge".[1] Theoretically, the design of this dredging tool was seriously flawed, as the heavy siltation of the lower Yellow River was caused by the sediment content of the river water exceeding the load of the current. In such circumstances, if the sediment-carrying capacity of the current could not be increased, even if the silt was stirred up, it would quickly settle not far away and would have no effect on deepening the riverbed, so this attempt to dredge sediment was an inevitable failure. Nevertheless, this guiding philosophy of river management, which places importance on the removal of silt from the riverbed, and the courageous spirit of exploration is worthy of full recognition, as it set the precedent for Chinese people to try to solve the siltation problem of the Yellow River by mechanical force nearly a thousand years ago.

The river was a constant source of trouble and gave rise to many ideas for river management, the most famous of which was Jia Rang's "Three Strategies for River Regulation". Jia's first best strategy was to divert the river artificially. At that time, the riverbed in the lower reaches of the Yellow River was already silted up, and in some places the water rose above the houses outside the embankment during high water, making it a typical overhanging river. The idea of artificial diversion was therefore based on the understanding of the root cause of the Yellow River's

---

[1] Xin Deyong. The History of the Yellow River [M]. Beijing. Social Science Literature Press, 2013:112.

分流派在明代曾长期占据优势地位，从明初到嘉靖年间，几乎所有治河者都主张分流以杀水势，这一派的代表人物有宋濂、徐有贞、白昂、刘大夏、刘天和等人，其中许多人不仅是徒有议论，而是身为治河官员，进行了相当规模的实践。然而，分流不但没有使河患减少，反而加重了淤积，加深了黄河的灾害。

鉴于明朝人分流治河失败的教训，清朝基本上不再有人重提这一主张，只有吏部尚书孙嘉淦在乾隆年间提出了一个分洪方案，虽然也是分流，但意在削减洪峰水势，减小灾害，比较符合实际。明代后期的万恭、潘季驯等人开始侧重于治沙，强调河流增强水势，以水攻沙，减少淤积，从而通畅下泄流路，消除水患。这样，独流与分流之争，就演变成了治水与治沙的分歧，这时的独流派已成为与大多数治河方略都不相同的治沙派。

潘季驯石雕
A Stone Sculpture of Pan Jixun

潘季驯吸取前人治河的经验教训，认识到治河必须治沙，为此他与

problems. The second best strategy of Jia Rang was to divert the river water, that is, to divert part of the water flow northward along the front edge of the alluvial fan of the Taihang Mountains and divert canals from it for irrigation. Through this way, the water volume of the Yellow River mainstream could be diverged. Where there was droght, it could be used for irrigation. When there was flood, it coud be used to lead off the flood, preventing over flowing of the mainstream. Meanwhlie, the branches diverged could also be used as shipping channel. This idea, as a river management strategy, can be called "diversion". The last choice of Jia Rang was to follow the general approach of raising and thickening the original embankments and maintaining the existing river. [1]

  The grop advocating diversion had occupied a favorable position during the Ming Dynasty. From the early Ming Dynasty to the Jiajing period, almost all of the riverkeepers advocated diversions to stem the flow of water, a school of thought represented by Song Lian, Xu Youzhen, Bai Ang, Liu Daxia, Liu Tianhe and others, many of whom were not just talking in vain, but were river officials and carried out considerable practice. However, instead of making the river less troubled, the diversions increased siltation and deepened the Yellow River's disasters.

  In view of the lessons learned from the failure of the Ming Dynasty in diverting rivers, this idea was basically no longer revisited in the Qing Dynasty, except for the Minister of Officials, Sun Jiagan, who proposed a flood diversion scheme during the Qianlong reign, which, still a kind of diverging plan, was intended to reduce the flooding potential and minimize disasters and was more realistic. In the late Ming Dynasty, Wan Gong, Pan Jixun and others began to focus on sand control, emphasizing that rivers enhance water potential, control sand with water and reduce siltation, thus opening up the downstream flow path and eliminating flooding. In this way, the debate between the solitary stream and the divergent stream evolved into a disagreement between water management and sand management. By this time solitary stream school had become a school of sand management that differed from most river management strategies.

---

[1] Xin Deyong. The History of the Yellow River [M]. Beijing: Social Science Literature Press,2013:121-122.

万恭等人反对当时盛行的分流治河主张，主张水流合而不分以增大水势，"以河治河，以水攻沙"[1]，即通过水流把泥沙冲下入海，减少河道的淤积。为此，他特别强调河堤的作用，因为通过堤防缩紧河道，河水就能加快流速，提高挟沙能力。经过潘季驯合流、筑堤束水之后，泥沙淤积在一定程度上确实有所减弱，十余年间没有发生大规模决溢。潘季驯也因为提出束水攻沙理论而颇受后人的钦佩，从此，黄河治理工程中便比较普遍地重视以水攻沙。

同时，人们也逐渐意识到，引起黄河下游河道泥沙淤积的根源是中游黄土高原地区严重的水土流失，如果只是把眼光盯在下游发生水患的河段，不去追溯整治泥沙的来源，很难彻底解决问题。经过长期探索，终于在清代中期的乾隆年间，一个叫胡定的御史意识到了这个重要问题，提出了治理中游泥沙流失的水土保持方案。他敏锐地观察到黄河中游所含的泥沙绝大多数出自三门峡以上的中游河段，于是提出了一个被称为"汰沙澄源"的水土保持方案。具体办法是在黄土高原沟壑区的沟涧口上筑坝，拦截洪水，把泥沙淤积在沟底，利用肥沃的淤泥种植小麦等农作物，这样既减少了水土流失，又有利于农业生产，一举两得。胡定提出的这种水土保持办法，现在一般称为"淤地坝"，这种修筑淤地坝的办法至今仍然是黄河中游水土保持最基本的手段之一，效果相当显著。胡定当年把这一建议呈交朝廷之后，主事者以"古未有行之者"为由，根本不假思索就将其否定掉了。[2]

一直到清朝灭亡，进入民国以后，人们才重新认识到，胡定在200年前所提出的这一见识是高明的。在治理黄河的工作中，人们开始重视中游地区的水土保持，并把筑造淤地坝作为重要的手段之一，大力进行推广。除了淤地坝之外，在水土保持方面，还有沟洫、梯田、种草、植

---

[1] 辛德勇.黄河史话[M].北京：社会科学文献出版社，2013:147.

[2] 辛德勇.黄河史话[M].北京：社会科学文献出版社，2013:150.

Learning from experience and the lessons of our predecessors in river control, Pan Jixun realized that river regulation must include sand regulation. For this reason, he and Wan Gong and others opposed the prevailing idea of diverting the flow of the river, advocating that the water flow should be combined but not divided to increase the water potential, and that "the river should be regulated by the river, and the sand should be regulated by the water", [1] which was to reduce the siltation of the river by washing the sediment down into the sea by the current. To this end, he particularly emphasized the role of the river embankment, as it was through the embankment that the river could be tightened to increase the river's velocity and improve its ability to carry sand. After Pan Jixun's combination of flow and dike construction, the siltation did weaken to a certain extent, and no large-scale overflow occurred for more than ten years, and Pan Jixun was admired by his descendants for his theory of regulating sand with water. Since then, it has become more common for the Yellow River regulation project to focus on the use of water to control sand.

At the same time, people were gradually realizing that the source cause of sediment accumulation in the lower reaches of the Yellow River was the serious soil erosion in the middle reaches of the Loess Plateau. It would be difficult to solve the problem completely if the focus was only on the downstream section of the river where the flooding occurred, without tracing the source of the sediment. After a long period of exploration, finally in the mid-Qing Dynasty, during the Qianlong period, an imperial official called Hu Ding realized this important problem and proposed a soil and water conservation plan to combat sediment loss in the middle reaches. He keenly observed that most of the sediment in the middle reaches of the Yellow River came from the middle reaches of the river above Sanmenxia, so he proposed a water and soil conservation program called "Sand Elimination at Its Source". The specific method was to dam the mouths of the gullies and streams in the Loess Plateau gullies to intercept flood water, silt the sediment at the bottom of the gullies and use the fertile silt to grow wheat and other crops, thus reducing soil erosion and facilitating agricultural production,

---

[1] Xin Deyong. The History of the Yellow River [M]. Beijing: Social Science Literature Press, 2013:147.

树等许多手段目前都已在黄土高原各地广泛实施,对于减少黄河泥沙含量起到了重要作用。

　　民国时期,由于战争和陡坡开荒等原因,森林草原遭到严重破坏,水土流失日益加剧,下游河道淤积严重。李仪祉、张含英等治黄专家在深入研究历代治黄方略的基础上,结合西方的科学技术,认识到黄河河患的症结在于泥沙,泥沙的根源在于水土流失。在李仪祉的《黄河治本计划概要叙目》和张含英的《黄河治理纲要》中,都把水土保持作为治黄之本,并提出了治理坡耕地、荒地与沟壑的具体措施,把水土保持正式纳入治黄计划。同时,围绕水土保持工作,进行了调查研究,提出了治理方案,建立了组织机构,开展了科学实验和小范围示范推广。虽然在当时的历史条件下,不可能大规模地开展,但把水土保持纳入治黄事业,作为治黄的主要方略,是认识上的一次飞跃。

李仪祉
Li Yizhi

　　1946年2月,晋冀鲁豫边区政府决定成立冀鲁豫解放区治河委员会,

killing two birds with one stone. This method of soil and water conservation proposed by Hu Ding is now commonly referred to as "silt dams", and is still one of the most basic means of soil and water conservation in the middle reaches of the Yellow River, with remarkable results. When Hu Ding submitted his proposal to the court, it was dismissed without a second thought, on the grounds that "it had never been done before". [1]

It was only after the fall of the Qing Dynasty and the advent of the Republic of China that people regained awareness of the remarkable insight that Hu Ding had put forward 200 years ago. In the efforts to manage the Yellow River, they attached importance to soil and water conservation in the middle reaches of the river and promoted the construction of silt dams as one of the important means of this measure. In addition to silt dams, many other means of soil and water conservation, such as ditching, terracing, grass planting and tree planting, have now been widely implemented throughout the Loess Plateau and have played an important role in reducing the sediment content of the Yellow River.

During the Republican period, due to war and steep slope clearing, forests and grasslands were severely damaged, soil erosion was increasing and the downstream river was heavily silted up. Li Yizhi, Zhang Hanying and other Yellow River experts, based on their in-depth study of Yellow River regulation strategies over the ages, combined with Western science and technology, realized that the crux of the Yellow River's problems lay in the siltation, and that the root cause of the siltation was soil erosion. Li Yizhi's *Outline of the Yellow River Treatment Plan* and Zhang Hanying's *Outline of the Yellow River Treatment*, both took soil and water conservation as the root of the Yellow River regulation, and proposed specific measures to treat sloping land, wasteland and ditching, formally incorporating soil and water conservation into the Yellow River regulation plan. At the same time, research and studies were carried out around soil and water conservation, regulation plans were proposed, organizations were established, scientific experiments and small-scale demonstrations were carried out and promoted. Although it was not possible on a large scale under the

---

[1] Xin Deyong. The History of the Yellow River [M]. Beijing: Social Science Literature Press, 2013:150.

这是中国共产党领导的第一个人民治理黄河机构。不久，为了加强对黄河故道两岸治河复堤工作的组织领导，冀鲁豫行署又决定将冀鲁豫解放区治河委员会改名为冀鲁豫黄河水利委员会，这就是今天"黄河水利委员会"的前身，从此掀开了人民治黄的新篇章。初期的黄河水利委员会在中国共产党的领导下，一手拿枪，一手拿锹，打赢了江苏坝保卫战、昆山抢险、高村抢险等一个个硬仗，完成了黄河归故后堤防不决口的艰巨任务。1949年6月16日，华北、华东、中原三解放区联合性的治黄机构——黄河水利委员会在山东省济南市成立。

2. 新中国黄河流域生态保护的成效

新中国成立以来，人民治理黄河不仅产生了巨大的经济效益，而且明显改善了流域及临黄地区的生态环境，有力促进了国家经济社会快速稳定发展，生态效益显著。新中国成立后，中国共产党和人民政府重视水土保持工作。1951年3月，周恩来总理亲自批示正式开工建设引黄工程，次年4月成功开闸放水，短短一年时间就成功建成了人民胜利渠，成为新中国成立以来在黄河下游兴建的第一座引黄灌溉工程。人民胜利渠建成七十年来，党中央领导人民充分开发利用水沙资源、发展引黄灌溉，把低洼荒凉的盐碱地变成了高产稳产的良田，豫北大地逐步发展成为中原粮仓，如闻名全国的"延津小麦""原阳大米"等。水是生命之源，生产之要，生态之基。人民胜利渠的建设使体弱多病的黄河逐步变成了生态文明的黄河，流域水生态环境也得到了逐步改善。

1952年，毛泽东视察黄河时看到黄河多泥沙，开始了解黄土高原水土保持的情况。同年12月，政务院发出《中央人民政府政务院关于发动群众继续开展防旱、抗旱运动并大力推行水土保持工作的指示》，对全国各地的水土保持工作做出了全面部署，黄河流域大规模的水土保持工作从此开启。修建水土保持工程和植树造林，进行重点治理，取得了很好的成效。据1957年统计，截至1956年底，配合农业、水利等措施，

historical conditions of the time, it was a leap of understanding to incorporate soil and water conservation into the cause of the Yellow River regulation as the main strategy.

In February 1946, the Shanxi-Hebei-Shandong-Henan Border Region Government decided to set up the Hebei-Shandong-Henan Liberated Area River Management Committee, which was the first people's organization to regulate the Yellow River under the leadership of the Chinese Communist Party. Soon after, in order to strengthen the organization and leadership of river management and dam restoration work in the old Yellow River course, the Hebei-Shandong-Henan Executive Office decided to rename the Hebei-Shandong-Henan Liberation Area River Control Commission as Hebei-Shandong-Henan Yellow River Water Conservancy Commission, which was the predecessor of today's "Yellow River Water Conservancy Commission", thus opening up a new chapter of the people's management of the Yellow River. Under the leadership of the CPC, the Yellow River Water Conservancy Commission won the battle of protecting Jiangsu Dam, rescuing Kunshan and Gaocun, and completed the difficult task of keeping the dykes from breaking after the Yellow River returned to its old course. On June 16, 1949, the Yellow River Water Conservancy Committee, a joint body for the management of the Yellow River in the three liberated areas of North China, East China and the Central Plains, was established in Jinan, Shandong Province. [1]

2. The Effectiveness of Ecological Conservation in the Yellow River Basin after the founding of the PRC

Since the founding of the PRC, the people's management of the Yellow River has not only produced huge economic benefits, but has also significantly improved the ecological environment of the watershed and the adjacent Yellow River area, which has contributed to the rapid and stable development of the country's economy and society. After the founding of the PRC, the Communist Party of China and the People's Government attached importance to soil and water conservation work. In March 1951, Premier Zhou Enlai personally approved the

---

[1] Introduction to the Yellow River Commission, Yellow River Net - Yellow River Conservancy Commission, Ministry of Water Resources.

黄河流域已控制水土流失面积达26000余平方千米，特别是造林、育林较早的地区，效果更为显著。

河南人民胜利渠
People's Victory Canal in Henan Province

1978年十一届三中全会以后，黄河流域水土保持工作掀开了新的一页。1982年8月16日至22日，全国水土保持工作协调小组在北京召开了全国第四次水土保持工作会议，钱正英总结了新中国成立以来水土保持的经验教训。从总体上看，20世纪80年代是黄河流域水土保持稳定发展和效果最好的时期。

第一，治理水土流失方面取得了突出的成绩。据黄河水利委员会农村水利水土保持局统计，从1950年至1991年，黄河流域8省（区）累计完成梯田、条田5081.95万亩，坝地449.12万亩，其他基本农田206.52万亩，造林11937.57万亩，种草3161.09万亩，五项主要措施共治理面积2.08亿多亩，折合13.89万平方千米，占黄河流域水土流失面积44万平方千米的31.6%。此外，还建成水窖、涝池、沟头防护、谷坊、陂塘等辅助性小型工程400多万处（座）。

第二，在减沙效益方面取得了突出成绩。黄河水利委员会水文局

official start of construction of the Yellow River Diversion Project, and in April of the following year, the gates were successfully opened and water released. In just one year, the People's Victory Canal was successfully completed, becoming the first irrigation project built in the lower reaches of the Yellow River since the founding of the PRC. Over the past 70 years since the completion of the People's Victory Canal, the Party Central Committee has led people to fully exploit the water and sand resources and develop irrigation by diverting yellow water, turning the low-lying and desolate saline land into high-yielding and stable fields, for example, the nationally renowned "Yanjin wheat" and "Yuanyang rice". Water is the source of life, the key to production and the foundation of ecology. The construction of the People's Victory Canal has gradually transformed the frail and sickly Yellow River into an ecological and civilized river, and the water ecology of the basin has been gradually improved.

In 1952, Mao Zedong began to understand the situation of soil and water conservation on the Loess Plateau when he saw a lot of sediment in the Yellow River during his inspection. In December of the same year, the State Council issued the Instruction of the State Council of the Central People's Government on Mobilizing the Masses to Continue the Campaign to Prevent and Combat Drought and Vigorously Promote Soil and Water Conservation Work, which made comprehensive plans for soil and water conservation work throughout the country, and large-scale soil and water conservation work in the Yellow River Basin began from then on. The construction of soil and water conservation projects and the planting of trees and forests to carry out key treatments have achieved good results. According to 1957 statistics, by the end of 1956, together with agricultural and water conservancy measures, the Yellow River Basin had controlled soil erosion over 26,000 square kilometers. Especially in areas where afforestation and reforestation had taken place earlier, the results were even more remarkable.

After the Third Plenary Session of the Eleventh Central Committee in 1978, a new page was turned in the work of soil and water conservation in the Yellow River Basin. From August 16 to 22 in 1982, the National Coordination Group for Soil and Water Conservation held the Fourth National Conference on Soil and Water Conservation in Beijing, where Qian Zhengying summarized the lessons

整编的观测资料显示,黄河龙羊峡至三门峡区间实测平均年输沙量为:1950—1959 年 17.804 亿吨,1960—1969 年 17.045 亿吨,1970—1979 年 13.601 亿吨,1980—1989 年 7.996 亿吨。随着水土保持的开展,黄河泥沙有逐年减少的趋势。20 世纪 80 年代与 60 年代相比,平均每年减少泥沙 9.049 亿吨。80 年代的实测输沙量与 60 年代的流域产沙量相比,平均每年减少 11.806 亿吨。

第三,在生态效益方面,改善了地表径流状况、小气候和耕地土壤性质,减轻了洪、旱、霜、冻、风沙灾害,为农业生产创造了良好的生态环境。据测定,农田林网使小气候发生了三方面变化:一是降低了风速,减轻了流失。林带全年平均有效防风范围在 20 倍树高左右,在此范围内减风效能为 36%,在 7 倍树高处可达 41.8%。与旷野相比,夏季林带内可减少风蚀 40%,冬春季减少 22%—28%。二是提高了地温。在有效防护范围内,全年日均地表温度提高 0.4℃,防风最佳处提高 0.5℃,在树木末叶期可提高 1.5℃。三是减少了蒸发,土壤含水量增加。林带防护范围内全年水面蒸发较对照区减少 8.8%,作物生长的 6—9 月间减少 5.7%,春旱严重的 5 月减少 9.6%。坡耕地修成水平梯田以后,水土流失减轻 90% 以上,耕地土壤性质得到改善,有利于粮食高产。[1]

2001 年 3 月,黄河水利委员会在原有水土保持项目的基础上,正式启动了黄河水土保持生态工程。该工程是利用黄河上中游水土保持重点防治工程投资,按照集中、重点、示范的原则实施的流域性水土保持生态建设标志工程。工程主要包括重点支流治理、示范区、小流域坝系工程、治沟骨干工程专项、生态修复、重点小流域等项目。"十五"期间,该工程共完成综合治理面积 6599.66 平方千米,共安排淤地坝 2832 座,其中骨干坝 735 座、中小型坝 2097 座;竣工验收淤地坝 1755 座,其中

---

[1] 王瑞芳.当代中国水利史(1949—2011)[M].北京:中国社会科学出版社,2014:491-493.

learned from soil and water conservation since the founding of New China. On the whole, the 1980s witnessed the steady development and best effects of soil and water conservation in the Yellow River Basin.

First, the prominent achievements have been made in the prevention of soil erosion. According to the statistics of the Bureau of Rural Water Conservancy and Soil Conservation of the Yellow River Conservancy Commission, from 1950 to 1991, a total of 50,819,500 mu of terraces and strip fields, 4,491,200 mu of dam land, 2,065,200 *mu* of other basic farmland, 119,375,700 *mu* of afforestation and 31,610,900 *mu* of grass planting were completed in eight provinces (provincial districts) in the Yellow River Basin. The five main measures have treated a total area of more than 208 million *mu*, equivalent to 138,900 square kilometers, accounting for 31.6% of the 440,000 square kilometers of soil erosion in the Yellow River Basin. In addition, more than 4 million small-scale projects, such as water cellars, flood ponds, ditch protection, check dams and ponds, have been built.

Second, outstanding achievements have been made in terms of sand reduction. According to the observations compiled by the Hydrological Bureau of the Yellow River Conservancy Commission, the measured average annual sand transport between Longyangxia and Sanmenxia of the Yellow River was 1.7804 billion tons in 1950—1959, 1.7045 billion tons in 1960—1969, 1.3601 billion tons in 1970—1979 and 799.6 million tons in 1980—1989. With the development of soil and water conservation, the Yellow River sediment has a tendency to decrease year by year. The average annual sediment reduction in the 1980s compared to the 1960s was 904.9 million tons. Measured sand transport in the 1980s compared to the basin sand production in the 1960s averaged a reduction of 1,180.6 million tons per year.

Third, in terms of ecological benefits, it has improved surface runoff conditions, microclimate and soil properties of arable land, reduced flood, drought, frost, freezing and wind-sand disasters, and created a good ecological environment for agricultural production. It has been tested that the farmland forestry network has led to three changes in microclimate: Firstly, it has reduced wind speed and mitigated erosion. The average effective wind protection range of the forest belt throughout the year is around 20 times the height of the trees, and

骨干坝241座、中小型坝1514座。黄河水土保持生态工程的实施，起到了很好的品牌示范作用，较大地改善了黄河流域水土流失区农村生产和生活条件，有效保护和改善了区域生态环境，入黄泥沙明显减少，有力地促进了区域经济社会的可持续发展，取得了显著的经济、社会、生态效益。"十五"期间，流域林草覆盖率提高了4.6%，每年可减少土壤流失量1.71亿吨，增加降水有效利用量30.59亿立方米。到2007年，黄土高原地区涌现出一批"沟里坝连坝，山上林草旺，家家有牛羊，户户有余粮"的富裕村庄，昔日的水土流失之地变成了山清水秀之乡。这得益于黄河上中游地区水土流失综合防治取得的新进展，特别是与黄土高原地区水土保持淤地坝试点工程建设的顺利推进密不可分。

在党和政府的高度重视和巨额资金扶助下，"十一五"时期黄河流域水土保持工作续写新篇章。2005—2010年的5年间，黄河流域共开展水土流失综合治理面积559万多平方千米，全流域累计初步治理水土流失面积达22万多平方千米。综合治理规模显著扩大，各种防护能力大幅提升，治理区群众的生产、生活条件和生态环境明显改善。年均减少入黄泥沙3.5亿至4.5亿吨，减缓了下游河床的淤积（抬高），为促进流域经济社会的发展发挥了重要作用。[1]

值得一提的是，经过多年治理，黄河实现了连续23年不断流，维护了黄河生命健康。黄河频繁的季节性断流始于20世纪70年代初，1997年断流最为严重，断流时间超过200天，断流河段长达704千米。黄河断流不仅制约中国经济社会发展，还加重了严重的水体污染与水环境的恶化、河口湿地生态系统的退化和生物多样性的衰减等重大生态环境问题。从1999年黄委会实施黄河干流水量统一调度以来，通过综合运用行政、法律、工程等手段，优化水资源配置，基本满足了沿黄湿地

---

[1] 王瑞芳.当代中国水利史（1949—2011）[M].北京：中国社会科学出版社，2014:628-629.

the wind reduction effectiveness is 36% in this range and up to 41.8% at 7 times the height of the trees. Compared to open fields, wind erosion can be reduced by 40% in summer and 22%—28% in winter and spring within the forest belt. Secondly, the ground temperature is increased. Within the effective protection zone, the average daily surface temperature increases by 0.4℃ throughout the year, 0.5℃ within the region under best protection and up to 15℃ in the late leaf stage of the trees. Thirdly, evaporation is reduced and soil water content is increased. The evaporation from the water surface within the forest belt protection is reduced by 8.8% throughout the year compared to the control area, by 5.7% between June and September when crops are growing, and by 9.6% in May when spring droughts are severe. After the sloping land was terraced horizontally, soil erosion was reduced by more than 90% and the soil properties of the cultivated land were improved, which was conducive to high food production. [1]

In March, 2001, the Yellow River Water Conservancy Commission officially launched the Yellow River Soil and Water Conservation Ecological Project on the basis of the original soil and water conservation project. Invested by the Upper and Middle Reaches of the Yellow River Water and Soil Conservation Key Prevention and Control Project, it is a watershed water and soil conservation ecological construction landmark project implemented in accordance with the principles of concentration, focus and demonstration. The project mainly includes key tributary management, demonstration areas, small watershed dam system projects, special ditch management backbone projects, ecological restoration, key small watersheds and other projects. During the "Tenth Five-Year Plan" period, the project completed a total comprehensive treatment area of 6,599.66 square kilometers, and arranged a total of 2,832 silt dams, including 735 backbone dams and 2,097 small and medium-sized dams; 1,755 silt dams were completed and accepted, including 241 backbone dams and 1,514 small and medium-sized dams. The implementation of the Yellow River Soil and Water Conservation Ecological Project has played a very good brand demonstration role, which has greatly improved the production and living conditions of rural areas in the Yellow River

---

[1] Wang Ruifang. History of contemporary Chinese water resources (1949-2011) [M]. Beijing: China Social Sciences Press, 2014:491-493.

补水需求，河流湿地面积增加，生物多样性明显提升，河道基本生态功能得以维持。水土流失综合防治成效显著，生态环境明显改善。至今为止，黄河已经实现连续23年不断流。相关水利部门大力推进生态保护修复，完善治理体系，全力守护黄河的生命健康。

黄河流域的水质状况得到改善，黄河的生态功能逐步恢复。"黄河宁，天下平。"新中国成立以来，在中国共产党的领导下，通过推进标准化堤防建设，综合采取修建水库、淤地坝、水平梯田等工程措施以及退耕还林还草等生物措施，开展了全流域水资源调控，大幅度减少了泥沙入河量，缓解了下游河床不断淤积抬升的严峻局面，在黄河治理与水生态保护方面取得了巨大成就。

在长期的水土流失治理实践中，黄土高原地区探索形成了以小流域为单元，山水田林路统一规划，梁峁沟坡塬综合治理，植物、工程、农耕措施优化配置的水土流失治理技术路线，已成为中国水土流失防治体系中一条重要的技术路线。

为了对黄河流域治理开发与保护进行总体部署，水利部组织黄委会和沿黄九省（区）编制了《黄河流域综合规划（2012—2030年）》。《规划》阐述了黄河流域的自然概况、流域经济社会发展布局及要求等问题，梳理了流域治理开发与保护取得的辉煌成就，同时也指出了当前及今后一段时期，黄河治理开发与保护面临的主要问题，如防洪防凌形势严峻、水资源供需矛盾尖锐、水土流失防治任务艰巨、水污染防治和水生态环境保护任重道远、水沙调控体系不完善、流域综合管理相对薄弱等。《规划》从总体上明确了黄河治理开发与保护的长远目标：维持黄河健康生命，谋求黄河长治久安，支撑流域经济社会可持续发展。在此基础上，具体对水沙调控体系、防洪减淤、水土保持、水资源开发利用、水资源与水生态环境保护、干流梯级工程布局和水力发电、岸线利用和干流航运、主要支流、流域综合管理和科技支撑体系等方面分别进行了规划安排。2013年3月，国务院在对《黄河流域综合规划（2012—2030年）》的

Basin soil erosion area, effectively protected and improved the regional ecological environment, and significantly reduced the inflow of sediment into the Yellow River, which has strongly promoted the sustainable development of regional economy and society and achieved significant economic, social and ecological benefits. During the "Tenth Five-Year Plan" period, the basin forest and grass cover increased by 4.6%, which can reduce soil loss by 171 million tons per year and increase the effective use of precipitation by 3.059 billion cubic meters. By 2007, the Loess Plateau region emerged a number of rich villages with "dams in the ditch, forest and grass on the mountain, cattle and sheep in every family, and surplus food in every household", and the former land of soil erosion has become a township of clear water and mountains. This is due to the new progress of comprehensive prevention and control of soil erosion in the upper and middle reaches of the Yellow River, especially with the smooth promotion of the pilot project of soil and water conservation silt dams in the Loess Plateau area.

With the high attention of the CPC and the government and huge financial support, the "Eleventh Five-Year Plan" period of the river basin soil and water conservation work continued to make new achievements. In the five years from 2005 to 2010, the Yellow River Basin has carried out comprehensive soil erosion management in an area of more than 5.59 million square kilometers, and the total area of preliminary soil erosion in the basin has reached more than 220,000 square kilometers. The scale of comprehensive treatment has been significantly expanded, various protective capacities have been greatly enhanced, the production and living conditions and ecological environment of the people in the treatment area have been significantly improved, the annual average reduction of human yellow sediment is 350 million to 450 million tons, and the siltation of the downstream riverbed has been slowed down, playing an important role in promoting the economic and social development of the basin. [1]

It is worth mentioning that after years of management, the Yellow River has achieved 23 consecutive years of non-stop flow, maintaining the life and health of the Yellow River. The frequent seasonal disruptions of the Yellow River began

---

[1] Wang Ruifang. History of Contemporary Chinese Water Resources (1949-2011) [M]. Beijing: China Social Sciences Press, 2014:628-629.

批复中明确了其实施要以完善黄河水沙调控、防洪减淤、水资源合理配置与高效利用、水土流失综合防治、水资源与水生态环境保护、流域综合管理体系为目标，坚持全面规划、统筹兼顾、标本兼治、综合治理，注重科学治水，为实现经济持续健康发展和社会和谐稳定提供有力支撑。《规划》是黄河流域开发、利用、节约、保护水资源和防治水害的重要依据，黄河流域的综合治理与开发也将随着对规划的具体实施而进一步展开，从而切实保障流域防洪安全、供水安全、粮食安全和生态安全。

党的十八大以来，以习近平同志为核心的党中央提出并深入贯彻创新、协调、绿色、开放、共享的新发展理念，生态文明建设被纳入中国特色社会主义事业"五位一体"的总体布局。习近平总书记围绕系统治水做出一系列重要论述和部署，提出了"节水优先、空间均衡、系统治理、两手发力"的治水方针，统筹做好水灾害防治、水资源节约、水生态保护修复和水环境治理，突出了治水的综合性。习近平总书记指明了用途管制和生态修复必须遵循自然规律以及对山水林田湖进行统一保护、统一修复的必要性，统筹兼顾、协调各方，把局部问题放在整个生态系统中来解决、来实现。党的十八大以来，习近平总书记多次考察黄河流域生态保护和修复工作，就水土保持生态建设做出一系列重要指示批示，为黄河流域水土保持工作提供了根本遵循。截至2019年底，在各级党委、政府领导和有关部门的大力支持下，经过广大人民群众的不懈努力和艰苦奋斗，黄河流域累计治理水土流失面积22万多平方千米，水土流失强度明显降低，入黄泥沙大幅减少，综合防治取得了显著成效，水土流失严重局面初步扭转。根据2019年全国水土流失动态监测结果，黄河流域尚有水土流失面积26.42万平方千米，人为水土流失恶化趋势得到有效遏制。2010年以来，黄河流域共6万个项目实施了水土保持方案，

in the early 1970s, and the most serious disruptions occurred in 1997, with a disruption time of more than 200 days and a disrupted river section of 704 km. The Yellow River cut off not only restricts the economic and social development of China, but also aggravates the serious water pollution and deterioration of water environment, degradation of estuarine wetland ecosystem and decay of biodiversity and other major ecological and environmental problems. Since 1999, when the Yellow River Committee implemented the unified scheduling of water in the main stream, through the comprehensive use of administrative, legal and engineering means to optimize the allocation of water resources, it has basically met the water replenishment needs of wetlands along the Yellow River, increased the area of river wetlands, significantly improved biodiversity and maintained the basic ecological functions of the river. The comprehensive prevention and control of soil erosion has been effective, and the ecological environment has improved significantly. So far, the Yellow River has achieved 23 consecutive years of non-stop flow. The relevant water conservancy departments vigorously promote ecological protection and restoration, improve the governance system, and make every effort to guard the life and health of the Yellow River.

The water quality condition of the Yellow River Basin has been improved, and the ecological function of the Yellow River has been gradually restored. "The Yellow River is at peace; the society is at peace." Since the founding of the PRC, under the leadership of the CPC, through the promotion of standardized embankment construction, the comprehensive adoption of engineering measures such as the construction of reservoirs, siltation dams and horizontal terraces, as well as biological measures such as returning farmland to forests and grasses, we have carried out basin-wide water resource control, significantly reduced the amount of sediment entering the river, alleviated the severe situation of continuous siltation and uplifting of the riverbed downstream, and made great achievements in the management of the Yellow River and water ecology protection.

In the long-term practice of soil erosion control, the Loess Plateau region has explored and formed a technical route of soil erosion control with small watersheds as units, unified planning of mountains, water, fields, forests and roads, comprehensive control of the slopes and plateaus of the mountains and the earth, and optimal configuration of plant, engineering and farming measures, which has

黄河源区支流黑河湿地——青海玛多县

become an important technical route in China's soil erosion control system.

In order to be able to scientifically develop an overall plan for the management, development and protection of the Yellow River Basin, the Ministry of Water Resources (MWR) has organized the Yellow River Basin Development and Conservation Commission and the nine provinces (provincial districts) along the Yellow River to formulate The Comprehensive Plan for the Yellow River Basin (2012–2030). The Plan sets out the natural profile of the Yellow River Basin, the layout and requirements of the economic and social development of the basin, and outlines the glorious achievements made in the management, development and protection of the basin. It also points out the major problems in the managent, development and protection of the Yellow River for now and for the days to come, such as severe situation of flood prevention and ice flood prevention, sharp contradiction between supply and demand of water resources, tough task of soil erosion contol, long-term water pollution managemet and water ecological environment, imcorrplete water and sedimet regulation system, and relatively weak comprehensive management of the Basin. The Plan defines the long-term peace and objectives of the development and protection of the Yellow River in general: to maintain the healthy and life of the Yellow River, to seek its long-term peace and stability, and to support the sustainable economic and social development of the river basin. On this basis, specific planning arrangements have been made for the water and sand control system, flood control and silt reduction, soil and water conservation, water resources development and utilization, water resources and water ecology environmental protection, the layout of the mainstream gradient projects and hydropower generation, shoreline utilization and main-stream navigation, major tributaries, comprehensive management of the basin and scientific and technological support systems. In March 2013, the State Council approved The Comprehensive Plan for the Yellow River Basin (2012–2030), specifying that its implementation should aim to improve the regulation of water and sand in the Yellow River, flood control and siltation reduction, rational allocation and efficient use of water resources, comprehensive prevention and control of soil erosion, water resources and water ecology environmental protection, and an integrated management system for the basin. It should insist on comprehensive planning, co-ordination and balance, treat both the symptoms

防治水土流失面积 3.3 万平方千米，减少水土流失量 4 亿多吨。[1]晋、陕、内蒙古接壤地区大中型生产建设项目实现了水土保持有序监管，建成了西气东输、西电东送等一批水土保持生态文明示范工程。从源头减少入黄泥沙作用突出，黄土高原是黄河泥沙的主要来源区，其中多沙粗沙区占62.8%。通过实施小流域综合治理、坡耕地整治、淤地坝工程、退耕还林还草等水土保持重点工程，年均减少入黄泥沙量 4.35 亿吨，占近年减少入黄泥沙量的一半以上，其中淤地坝工程年均减少 1.5 亿—2 亿吨。持续改善生态环境成效显著，坡耕地整治、淤地坝等水土保持工程，进一步促进和巩固了退耕还林还草，有效提升了林草植被覆盖度，改善了区域生态环境。有力促进了经济社会发展，水土流失治理注重与脱贫攻坚、乡村振兴紧密结合，经济社会效益显著。据 2019 年调研评估，黄河流域现有梯田 477 万公顷，淤成坝地 8.58 万公顷。年新增粮食生产能力 3 亿公斤，累计解决了 150 多万山区人口吃粮问题，100 多万贫困人口稳定脱贫。同时培育出甘肃静宁苹果、定西马铃薯和陕西永寿核桃等一批特色产业，形成了陕西绥德辛店沟等一批乡村生态旅游基地，打造了山西朔州西山等一批休闲康养产业，有力促进了当地经济社会发展。

习近平总书记在 2019 年 9 月视察黄河期间召开的座谈会上明确提出了黄河流域生态保护和高质量发展重大战略，这一战略同京津冀协同发展、长江经济带发展、粤港澳大湾区建设、长三角一体化发展一样，是重大国家战略。讲话发表以来，全国水利系统迅速行动，黄河流域生态建设进入了一个新阶段。

一是水土保持政策规划逐步完善。2021 年 9 月，水利部研究制定了《推动黄河流域水土保持高质量发展的指导意见》，明确了"十四五"和今后一个时期，黄河流域水土保持工作的目标任务、重点举措和有关要求等。2021 年 10 月，中共中央、国务院印发了《黄河流域生态保护

---

[1] 张宝.新时期黄河流域水土流失防治对策[J].中国水土保持，2021(7).

and the root causes, use comprehensive management, focus on scientific water management, and provide strong support for achieving sustainable and healthy economic development and social harmony and stability. The Plan is an important basis for the development, utilization, conservation and protection of water resources and the prevention and control of water hazards in the Yellow River Basin. The comprehensive management and development of the Yellow River Basin will also be further developed with the concrete implementation of the Plan, so as to effectively guarantee the safety of flood control, water supply, food security and ecological safety of the basin.

Since the 18th CPC Congress, the Party Central Committee, with Comrade Xi Jinping at its core, has proposed and thoroughly implemented the new development concept of innovation, coordination, green, openness and sharing, and the construction of ecological civilization has been incorporated into the overall layout of the "Five-In-One" socialist cause with Chinese characteristics. General Secretary Xi Jinping has made a series of important comments and arrangements on systematic water management, and proposed the water management policy of "prioritizing water conservation, spatial balance, systematic management and two-handed efforts", which has highlighted the comprehensive nature of water management by coordinating water disaster prevention and control, water conservation, water ecology protection and restoration and water environment management. General Secretary Xi Jinping has indicated the need for use control and ecological restoration to follow the laws of nature and the need for unified protection and restoration of mountains, water, forests, fields and lakes. We should integrate and coordinate all parties, and place local problems in the context of the entire ecosystem to solve and achieve them. Since the 18th CPC Congress, General Secretary Xi Jinping has repeatedly inspected the ecological protection and restoration work in the Yellow River Basin and made a series of important instructions on the ecological construction of soil and water conservation, providing fundamental guidelines for the work of soil and water conservation in the Yellow River Basin. By the end of 2019, under the leadership of party committees and governments at all levels and the strong support of relevant departments, through the unremitting efforts and hard work of the general public, the Yellow River Basin has managed a cumulative total of more

三门峡天鹅湖（聂保华摄）

than 220,000 km² of soil erosion, with the intensity of soil erosion significantly reduced, the sediment entering the Yellow River significantly reduced, and comprehensive prevention and control has achieved remarkable results. The serious situation of soil erosion was initially reversed. According to the results of the national dynamic monitoring of soil erosion in 2019, the Yellow River Basin still has an area of 264,200 km² of soil erosion, and the deteriorating trend of human-induced soil erosion has been effectively curbed. Since 2010, a total of 60,000 projects in the Yellow River Basin have implemented soil and water conservation programs, preventing and controlling soil erosion over an area of 33,000 km² and reducing soil erosion by more than 400 million tons.[1] Large and medium-sized production and construction projects in the bordering areas of Shanxi, Shaanxi and Inner Mongolia have achieved orderly supervision of soil and water conservation, and a number of water and soil conservation and ecological civilization demonstration projects have been built, such as the West-East Gas Transmission and West-East Electricity Transmission. The Loess Plateau is the main source of sediment for the Yellow River, of which 62.8% is sandy and coarse sandy areas. Through the implementation of small watershed comprehensive management, sloping land remediation, silt dam projects, returning farmland to forest and grass and other key soil and water conservation projects, the annual average reduction in the amount of sediment entering the Yellow River is 435 million tons, accounting for more than half of the reduction in recent years, of which the average annual reduction in silt dam projects is 150-200 million tons. Continuous improvement of the ecological environment has been effective, with sloping land remediation, silt dams and other soil and water conservation projects further promoting and consolidating the return of cultivated land to forest and grass, effectively enhancing the forest and grass vegetation cover and improving the regional ecological environment. It has effectively promoted economic and social development, with soil erosion management focusing on close integration with poverty eradication and rural revitalization, with significant economic and social benefits. According to the 2019 research and assessment, the Yellow River

---

[1] Zhang Bao. Countermeasures of Soil Erosion Control in the Yellow River Basin in the new era [J]. China Soil and Water Conservation, 2021(7).

和高质量发展规划纲要》，并发出通知，要求各地区各部门结合实际认真贯彻落实。水利部按照"三对标、一规划"专项行动部署，组织编制了《黄河流域水土流失综合防治规划》。为深入贯彻总书记提出的"有条件的地方要大力建设旱作梯田、淤地坝等"重要指示精神，水利部会同国家发展改革委编制印发了《黄河流域淤地坝建设和坡耕地水土流失综合治理"十四五"实施方案》，拟通过5年时间，以中游黄土高原地区为重点，新建淤地坝1461座、拦沙坝2559座，实施坡改梯407万亩。工程实施后将对协调黄河水沙关系、保障黄河长治久安、改善流域生态环境发挥重要作用。

二是水土流失治理投入增幅明显。从现有投资渠道和规模来看，"十四五"时期，100%的中央预算内投资和55%的中央财政水利发展资金共250亿元安排到黄河流域相关省份，较"十三五"期间增长三分之二。其中，2021年已安排水土保持中央资金54.21亿元，占全国的70%。支持地方以增强水土保持能力为目标，以减少入河入库泥沙为重点，实施小流域综合治理、坡耕地综合整治、淤地坝和拦沙坝等水土保持重点工程，改善区域生态环境。

三是人为水土流失监管得到加强。《黄河流域生态保护和高质量发展规划纲要》明确要求实行最严格的生产建设活动监管。两年来，沿黄9省（区）各级水利部门坚持生态优先、绿色发展的理念，坚持问题导向和目标导向，组织开展了生产建设项目水土保持专项整治，重点整治"未批先建"、"未验先投"、未落实水土保持措施等6类水土保持违法违规行为。截至目前，黄委会和地方水利部门排查认定水土保持违法违规项目8286个，其中8272个项目已完成整改，整改率达到99.8%。通过严格监管和依法查处违法违规行为，有效遏制了人为水土流失，推动了黄河流域生态保护和高质量发展。

四是地方政府水土保持目标责任进一步落实。按照《黄河流域生态保护和高质量发展规划纲要》约束性指标，地方政府认真落实水土保持

Basin has 4.77 million hm² of existing terraced fields and 85,800 hm² of dammed silted land. The annual grain production capacity of 300 million kilograms has been added, and a total of more than 1.5 million mountain people have been solved to eat food, and more than 1 million poor people have been steadily lifted out of poverty. At the same time, it has cultivated a number of special industries such as apples in Jingning in Gansu, potatoes in Dingxi and walnuts in Yongshou in Shaanxi, formed a number of rural ecological tourism bases such as Xindiangou in Suide in Shaanxi, and created a number of leisure and recreation industries such as Xishan, Shuozhou in Shanxi, which have strongly promoted local economic and social development.

General Secretary Xi Jinping clearly proposed a major strategy for the ecological protection and high-quality development of the Yellow River Basin at a symposium held during his visit to the Yellow River in September 2019. This strategy is as significant a national strategy as the coordinated development of Beijing-Tianjin-Hebei, the development of the Yangtze River Economic Belt, the construction of the Guangdong-Hong Kong-Macao Greater Bay Area and the integrated development of the Yangtze River Delta. Since the speech was delivered, the national water conservancy system has acted swiftly and the ecological construction of the Yellow River Basin has entered a new phase.

First, the policy and planning of soil and water conservation has been gradually improved. In September 2021, the Ministry of Water Resources formulated the Guidance on Promoting High-Quality Development of Soil and Water Conservation in the Yellow River Basin, which clearly defined the objectives and tasks, key initiatives and requirements for soil and water conservation in the Yellow River Basin for the 14th Five-Year Plan and the next period. In October 2021, the Central Committee of the Communist Party of China (CPC) and the State Council triggered The Outline of the Plan for Ecological Protection and High-Quality Development of the Yellow River Basin and issued a notice requesting all regions and departments to seriously implement it in conjunction with the actual situation. The Ministry of Water Resources (MOWR), in accordance with the "three benchmarks and one plan", organized the preparation of The Comprehensive Prevention and Control Plan for Soil and Water Erosion in the Yellow River Basin. In order to carry out the

目标责任。水利部结合对省级人民政府实施全国水土保持规划情况评估,不断优化评估指标,通过评估进一步压实地方政府水土保持目标责任。同时加强黄河流域水土流失动态监测,定量掌握水土流失变化情况,研究制定有关对策。

五是水土保持相关基础工作扎实推进。为认真落实《黄河流域生态保护和高质量发展规划纲要》有关要求,水利部组织黄委会和黄土高原7省(区)对中型以上淤地坝开展风险隐患排查。组织黄委会研究制定《高标准淤地坝建设管理指南》,明确了高标准淤地坝的定义、标准和管理要求。同时,为适应新时期淤地坝建设管理需要,组织修订《黄土高原地区水土保持淤地坝工程建设管理办法》,研究制定《黄土高原地区淤地坝工程安全运用监督检查办法》《淤地坝登记销号管理规定》等制度。[1]

黄河流域水土流失面积和强度实现"双下降",生态环境持续向好,水土流失严重的状况明显好转。与1990年国务院第一次全国土壤侵蚀遥感调查结果相比,2020年黄河流域水土流失面积减少20.23万平方千米,减幅43.51%。其中,强烈及以上水土流失面积减幅81.70%,成效显著。截至2020年底,黄河流域累计初步治理水土流失面积25.24万平方千米,其中修建梯田608.02万公顷、营造水土保持林1263.54万公顷、种草234.30万公顷、封禁治理418.35万公顷;累计建成淤地坝5.81万座,其中大型淤地坝5858座、中型淤地坝1.2万座、小型淤地坝4.03万座。黄河流域水土保持率从1990年的41.49%、1999年的46.33%,提高到2020年的66.94%,其中黄土高原地区水土保持率63.44%。[2]

---

[1] 蒲朝勇.奋力推进黄河流域水土保持高质量发展[J].中国水利,2021(18).

[2] 参见《黄河流域水土保持公报(2020)》。

important instruction of the General Secretary that "dry terraces and silt dams should be built where possible", the Ministry of Water Resources, together with the National Development and Reform Commission, has prepared and issued The Implementation Plan for the Construction of Silt Dams and Comprehensive Management of Soil Erosion on Sloping Arable Land in the Yellow River Basin during the 14th Five-Year Plan Period. It is proposed that through five years, 1,461 new silt dams and 2,559 sand barrage dams will be built and 4.07 million *mu* of slope to ladder conversion will be implemented, focusing on the midstream Loess Plateau area. The project will play an important role in coordinating the relationship between water and sand in the Yellow River, ensuring the long-term stability of the Yellow River and improving the ecological environment of the river basin.

Second, the investment in soil erosion control has increased significantly. From the existing investment channels and scale, during the 14th Five-Year Plan period, 100% of the central budget investment and 55% of the central financial development funds for water conservancy totaling 25 billion yuan have been arranged to the relevant provinces in the Yellow River Basin, an increase of two thirds compared to the 13th Five-Year Plan period. Of these, RMB 5.421 billion, or 70% of the country's total, has been allocated for soil and water conservation in 2021. The project aims to enhance soil and water conservation capacity and to mainly reduce sediment entering rivers and reservoirs, and to improve the regional ecological environment through the implementation of key soil and water conservation projects such as integrated management of small watersheds, comprehensive improvement of sloping land, siltation dams and sand barrages.

Third, the regulation of man-made soil erosion has been strengthened. The Outline of the Plan for Ecological Protection and Quality Development of the Yellow River Basin clearly calls for the strictest supervision of production and construction activities. Over the past two years, water conservancy departments at all levels in the nine provinces (provincial districts) along the Yellow River have adhered to the concept of ecological priority and green development, and to the problem-oriented and target-oriented approach. Special rectification of water and soil conservation in production construction projects was organized. The focus is on rectifying six types of water and soil conservation violations, such as "building

年宝玉则峰下——青海久治

before approval", "investing before inspection" and failing to implement water and soil conservation measures. Up to now, the Yellow River Conservancy Committee and local water conservancy departments have identified 8,286 illegal projects for soil and water conservation, of which 8,272 projects have been rectified, with a rectification rate of 99.8%. Through strict supervision and legal investigation of violations, man-made soil erosion has been effectively curbed and ecological protection and high-quality development of the Yellow River Basin has been promoted.

Fourth, the local governments' responsibility for soil and water conservation targets was further implemented. In accordance with the binding indicators in The Outline of the Plan for Ecological Protection and Quality Development of the Yellow River Basin, local governments have conscientiously implemented their responsibilities for soil and water conservation targets. The Ministry of Water Resources, in conjunction with its assessment of the implementation of the National Soil and Water Conservation Plan by provincial people's governments, has continuously optimized the assessment indicators and further consolidated the responsibilities of local governments for soil and water conservation objectives through the assessment. At the same time, the Ministry of Water Resources has strengthened the dynamic monitoring of soil and water erosion in the Yellow River Basin to quantitatively grasp the changes in soil and water erosion and to study and formulate relevant countermeasures.

Fifth, the basic work related to soil and water conservation was solidly promoted. In order to conscientiously implement the relevant requirements of The Outline of the Plan for Ecological Protection and Quality Development of the Yellow River Basin, the Ministry of Water Resources organized the Yellow River Conservancy Committee and the seven provinces (provincial districts) of the Loess Plateau to carry out risk and hidden danger surveys on silt dams above medium size. The Ministry of Water Resources organized the Yellow River Conservancy Committee to study and formulate The Guidelines for the Construction and Management of High Standard Silt Dams, which clarifies the definition, standards and management requirements of high standard silt dams. At the same time, the Ministry of Water Resources, in order to meet the needs of the new era of silt dam construction and management, organized the revision

3. 新时代黄河流域生态保护的形势和任务

新时代黄河治理的相关战略部署，贯彻落实了创新、协调、绿色、开放、共享的新发展理念，有力推进了黄河流域生态保护和高质量发展。

习近平总书记一直非常关心黄河治理、重视黄河流域生态保护，不辞劳苦，亲自考察调研，沿黄九省（区）都留下了他的足迹。2019年9月17日，习近平总书记在河南省郑州市考察调研时参观了黄河博物馆，接着在黄河国家地质公园沿着黄河岸边步行视察周边环境，了解生态保护、水资源利用等情况。第二天上午，习近平总书记主持召开了黄河流域生态保护和高质量发展座谈会并发表重要讲话。他在讲话中全面总结了中华民族治黄史与黄河治理取得的成就，深入分析了黄河流域的突出困难和问题，发出"让黄河成为造福人民的幸福河"的号召，为新时代黄河流域生态保护和高质量发展擘画了宏伟的蓝图。[1] 黄河流域生态保护和高质量发展，同京津冀协同发展、长江经济带发展、粤港澳大湾区建设、长三角一体化发展并列，由此成为新时代的重大国家战略。[2] 习近平总书记提出的黄河流域生态保护和高质量发展战略，把握了新时代黄河流域发展的新需求，标志着黄河治理进入了新时代。"黄河宁，天下平"，保护黄河是事关中华民族伟大复兴和永续发展的千秋大计。新形势下，黄河流域的水生态保护被提到了一个全新的高度，如何打赢这场攻坚战役，是新时代赋予我们的新的历史使命。习近平总书记对黄河流域生态保护和高质量发展做了重要部署，他提出了主要目标任务：要坚持绿水青山就是金山银山的理念，坚持生态优先、绿色发展，以水而定、量水而行，因地制宜、分类施策，上下游、干支流、左右岸统筹谋划，共同抓好大保护，协同推进大治理，着力加强生态保护治理、保

---

[1]《求是》杂志编辑部.让黄河成为造福人民的幸福河[J].小康，2019(11).

[2] 习近平.在黄河流域生态保护和高质量发展座谈会上的讲话[J].求是，2019(20).

of The Loess Plateau Area Water and Soil Conservation Silt Dam Construction Management Measures, and researched and developed The Loess Plateau Area Silt Dam Project Safety Operation Supervision and Inspection Measures, The Silt Dam Registration and Cancellation Management Regulations and other systems.[1]

The area and intensity of soil erosion in the Yellow River Basin have been "doubly reduced", the ecological environment has continued to improve, and the situation of serious soil erosion has been significantly improved. Compared with the results of the first national soil erosion remote sensing survey conducted by the State Council in 1990, the area of soil erosion in the Yellow River Basin was reduced by 202,300 square kilometers in 2020, a 43.51% reduction. Among them, the area of strong and above soil erosion has been reduced by 81.70%, which is a remarkable result. By the end of 2020, the Yellow River Basin had initially managed a total of 252,400 square kilometers of soil erosion, including the construction of 6,080,200 hectares of terraces, 12,635,400 hectares of soil and water conservation forests, 2,343,000 hectares of grass, and 4,183,500 hectares of closed control. A total of 58,100 silt dams have been built, including 5,858 large silt dams, 12,000 medium silt dams and 40,300 small silt dams. The rate of soil and water conservation in the Yellow River Basin has increased from 41.49% in 1990 and 46.33% in 1999 to 66.94% in 2020, including 63.44% in the Loess Plateau.[2]

3. The Situation and Tasks of Ecological Protection in the Yellow River Basin in the New Era

The relevant strategic deployment of the Yellow River management in the new era has implemented the new development concept of innovation, coordination, green, openness and sharing, and has vigorously promoted the ecological protection and high-quality development of the Yellow River Basin.

General Secretary Xi Jinping has always been very concerned about the

---

[1] Pu Chaoyong. Striving to Promote the High-quality Development of Soil and Water Conservation in the Yellow River Basin [J]. China Water Conservancy, 2021(18).

[2] Report on Soil and Water Conservation in the Yellow River Basin (2020)

management of the Yellow River and the ecological protection of the Yellow River Basin and has gone to great lengths to personally investigate and research, leaving his footprints in all nine provinces (provincial districts) along the Yellow River. On September 17, 2019, General Secretary Xi Jinping visited the Yellow River Museum during his research in Zhengzhou City, Henan Province, followed by a walk along the banks of the Yellow River at the Yellow River National Geological Park to inspect the surrounding environment and learn about ecological protection and water resources utilization. The next morning, General Secretary Xi Jinping hosted a symposium on ecological protection and quality development of the Yellow River Basin and delivered an important speech. In his speech, he comprehensively summarized the history and achievements of the Yellow River and the achievements of the Yellow River, analyzed the outstanding difficulties and problems of the Yellow River Basin, and issued a call to "make the Yellow River a happy river for the people", drawing a grand blueprint for the ecological protection and quality development of the Yellow River Basin in the new era. [1] The ecological protection and quality development of the Yellow River Basin has become a major national strategy in the new era, alongside the coordinated development of Beijing-Tianjin-Hebei, the development of the Yangtze River Economic Belt, the construction of the Guangdong-Hong Kong-Macao Bay Area and the integrated development of the Yangtze River Delta. [2] The ecological protection and high-quality development strategy of the Yellow River Basin proposed by General Secretary Xi Jinping has grasped the new needs of the development of the Yellow River Basin in the new era, marking a new era of Yellow River regulation. "If the Yellow River is at peace, the world will be at peace." The protection of the Yellow River is a great plan for a thousand years for the great rejuvenation and sustainable development of the Chinese nation. Under the new situation, the protection of the water ecology of the Yellow River Basin has been brought to a whole new level, and how to win

---

[1] Editorial Department of Qiushi. Make the Yellow River a Happy River for the Benefit of the People[J]. Insight China, 2019(11).

[2] Xi Jinping. Speech at the Symposium on Ecological Protection and High-quality Development of the Yellow River Basin[J]. Qiushi, 2019(20).

障黄河长治久安、促进全流域高质量发展、改善人民群众生活、保护传承弘扬黄河文化，让黄河成为造福人民的幸福河。[1]为了深入贯彻习近平总书记重要讲话精神，2020年6月，河南省政协召开常委会议，围绕"加强黄河流域生态保护"专题协商议政。2021年9月29日，河南省十三届人大常委会第二十七次会议表决通过了《河南省人民代表大会常务委员会关于促进黄河流域生态保护和高质量发展的决定》，将高水平建设大河治理和生态保护示范区、水资源节约集约利用和现代农业发展先行区、高质量发展引领区、黄河文化优势彰显区。

2020年1月3日，习近平总书记主持召开了中央财经委员会第六次会议并发表重要讲话。他强调，黄河流域必须下大气力进行大保护、大治理，走生态保护和高质量发展的路子。会议还对编制好、落实好黄河流域生态保护和高质量发展规划提出了明确要求。

2020年8月31日，中共中央政治局召开会议，会上审议了《黄河流域生态保护和高质量发展规划纲要》。会议强调，要因地制宜、分类施策、尊重规律，改善黄河流域生态环境，促进全流域高质量发展。

2021年以来，政府围绕黄河流域生态保护出台了一系列相关政策。8月，国家发展改革委、住建部联合印发《"十四五"黄河流域城镇污水垃圾处理实施方案》；9月，水利部印发《关于实施黄河流域深度节水控水行动的意见》；10月8日，国务院常务会议通过了《中华人民共和国黄河保护法（草案）》。当天，中共中央、国务院印发了《黄河流域生态保护和高质量发展规划纲要》。《纲要》指出，要以习近平新时代中国特色社会主义思想为指导，坚持生态优先、绿色发展，坚持量水而行、节水优先，坚持因地制宜、分类施策，坚持统筹谋划、协同推进的主要原则，使黄河流域成为大江大河治理的重要标杆、国家生态安

---

[1] 习近平.在黄河流域生态保护和高质量发展座谈会上的讲话[J].求是，2019(20).

the battle is a new historical mission given to us in the new era. General Secretary Xi Jinping has made important arrangements for ecological protection and high-quality development of the Yellow River Basin, and he has put forward the main objectives and tasks: to adhere to the concept of green mountains and clear water are equal to mountains of gold and silver, adhere to ecological priority and green development. Decisions and actions should be made according to water quantity, policies should be implemented according to different situations. The Chinese people should plan the upstream and downstream, the mainstream and tributaries, the left and right banks in an integrated manner. Joint protection and joint governace should be advanced in coordination, so as to strengthen the ecological protection and governance. The government should protect the Yellow River for its long-term stability and high-quality development, improve people's lives, and promote the Yellow River culture, so as to make the Yellow River a happy river for the benefit of the people. [1] In order to thoroughly implement the requirements of General Secretary Xi's important speech, in June 2020, the Standing Committee of the Henan provincial CPPCC held a meeting to negotiate and discuss political affairs around the theme of "strengthening the ecological protection of the Yellow River Basin". On September 29, 2021, the 27th meeting of the Standing Committee of the 13th Henan Provincial People's Congress voted and adopted the Decision of Promoting Ecological Protection and High-Quality Development of the Yellow River Basin, which will build a high-level demonstration area for river governance and ecological protection, a pilot area for water resources conservation and intensive utilization and modern agricultural development, a leading area for high-quality development, and an area for highlighting the cultural advantages of the Yellow River.

On January 3, 2020, General Secretary Xi Jinping hosted the sixth meeting of the Central Finance and Economics Commission and delivered an important speech. He stressed that the Yellow River Basin must make great efforts to carry out major protection and treatment and take the path of ecological protection and high-quality development. The meeting also put forward clear requirements for

---

[1] Xi Jinping. Speech at the Symposium on Ecological Protection and High-quality Development of the Yellow River Basin[J]. Qiushi, 2019(20).

全的重要屏障、高质量发展的重要实验区和中华文化保护传承弘扬的重要承载区。《纲要》提出了阶段性的发展目标：到2030年，黄河流域人水关系进一步改善，流域治理水平明显提高等；到2035年，黄河流域生态保护和高质量发展取得重大战略成果，黄河流域生态环境得到全面改善等；到本世纪中叶，黄河流域物质文明、政治文明、精神文明、社会文明、生态文明水平大幅提升，在中国建成富强民主文明和谐美丽的社会主义现代化强国中发挥重要支撑作用。《纲要》明确了要建设上游水源涵养能力、加强中游水土保持、推进下游湿地保护和生态治理，具体通过加强全流域水资源节约集约利用、全力保障黄河长治久安、强化环境污染系统治理、建设特色优势现代产业体系、构建区域城乡发展新格局、加强基础设施互联互通、保护传承弘扬黄河文化、补齐民生短

the preparation and implementation of a good ecological protection and high-quality development plan for the Yellow River Basin.

On August 31, 2020, the Political Bureau of the Central Committee of the Communist Party of China held a meeting at which it discussed The Outline of the Plan for Ecological Protection and High-Quality Development of the Yellow River Basin. The meeting stressed the need to improve the ecological environment of the Yellow River Basin and promote high-quality development in the whole basin by taking into account local conditions, classifying policies and respecting the laws.

Since 2021, a series of relevant policies have been introduced around the ecological protection of the Yellow River Basin. In August, the National Development and Reform Commission and the Ministry of Housing and Construction jointly issued "The Implementation of Urban Sewage and Waste Treatment Plan in the Yellow River Basin" during the 14th Five-Year Plan Period. In September, the Ministry of Water Resources issued The Opinions on the Implementation of Deep Water Conservation and Water Control Actions in the Yellow River Basin. On October 8, the State Council executive meeting adopted The Draft Law of the People's Republic of China on the Protection of the Yellow River. On the same day, the Central Committee of the Communist Party of China and the State Council issued The Outline of the Plan for the Ecological Protection and Quality Development of the Yellow River Basin. The Plan states that it should be guided by Xi Jinping's thought of socialism with Chinese characteristics in the new era, adhere to ecological priority and green development. The Chinese people should adhere to the main principles of water measurement and water conservation, adapt to local conditions and implement policies according to different categories, plan in an integrated manner and promote in a coordinated manner. They should make the Yellow River Basin an important benchmark for the regulation of large rivers, an important barrier for national ecological security, an important experimental area for high-quality development and an important bearing area for the preservation and heritage promotion of Chinese culture. The above outline sets out phased development goals: by 2030, the relationship between people and water in the Yellow River Basin will be further improved and the level of basin regulation will be

板和弱项、加快改革开放步伐等方面推进规划实施，确保在2025年前黄河流域生态保护和高质量发展取得明显进展。正式发布的《纲要》成为指导当前和今后一个时期黄河流域生态保护和高质量发展的纲领性文件，对指导沿黄地区立足新时代，贯彻新发展理念，推动黄河流域生态保护和高质量发展具有重大意义。10月22日，习近平总书记在济南主持召开深入推动黄河流域生态保护和高质量发展座谈会并发表重要讲话。他强调，要科学分析当前黄河流域生态保护和高质量发展形势，把握好推动黄河流域生态保护和高质量发展的重大问题，咬定目标、脚踏实地，埋头苦干、久久为功，确保"十四五"时期黄河流域生态保护和高质量发展取得明显成效，为黄河永远造福中华民族而不懈奋斗。

2020年3月至2022年5月，河南省黄河流域生态保护和高质量发展领导小组召开了六次会议，深入学习贯彻习近平总书记关于黄河流域生态保护和高质量发展的重要讲话重要指示，听取工作情况汇报，研究部署相关工作，致力于"让黄河成为造福人民的幸福河"，确保黄河流域生态保护和高质量发展在河南省不断取得新进展新成效。

2022年1月19日，中共中央政治局常委、国务院副总理、推动黄河流域生态保护和高质量发展领导小组组长韩正主持召开推动黄河流域生态保护和高质量发展领导小组全体会议。韩正指出，推动黄河流域生态保护和高质量发展，是以习近平同志为核心的党中央作出的重大决策部署。要牢牢把握共同抓好大保护、协同推进大治理的战略导向，全方位贯彻"四水四定"原则，始终坚持问题导向，推动黄河流域生态保护和高质量发展不断取得新进展。

当前，中国特色社会主义已进入新时代，治水兴水迎来了难得的战略新机遇。习近平总书记指出，治理黄河，重在保护，要在治理。黄河流域生态保护和高质量发展上升为国家战略，黄河沿岸将迈入生态保护和高质量发展新阶段。要在研究归纳前人治理黄河历程的基础上，贯彻落实新发展理念和新时期的治水方针，为脱贫攻坚、生态文明建设提供

significantly enhanced, etc. By 2035, significant strategic achievements in the ecological protection and high-quality development of the Yellow River Basin, and overall improvement in the ecological environment of the Yellow River Basin, etc. should be realized. By the middle of this century, the Yellow River Basin will have significantly improved its material, political, spiritual, social and ecological civilization, and will play an important supporting role in building a strong, democratic, civilized, harmonious and beautiful socialist modern state in China. The outline specifies the need to build water conservation capacity in the upper reaches, strengthen soil and water conservation in the middle reaches, and promote wetland protection and ecological management in the lower reaches. Specifically, the outline will be implemented by strengthening the economical and intensive use of water resources throughout the basin, ensuring the long-term stability of the Yellow River, strengthening the systematic management of environmental pollution, building a modern industrial system with special advantages, constructing a new pattern of regional urban and rural development, strengthening the interconnection of infrastructure, protecting the heritage and promoting the Yellow River culture, making up for the shortcomings and weaknesses of people's livelihood, and accelerating the pace of reform and opening up, to ensure that significant progress is made in ecological protection and high-quality development in the Yellow River Basin by 2025. The official release of the Outline has become a programmatic document to guide the ecological protection and high-quality development of the Yellow River Basin in the current and future period, which is of great significance in guiding the areas along the Yellow River based on the new era, implementing the new development concept and promoting the ecological protection and high-quality development of the Yellow River Basin. On October 22, General Secretary Xi Jinping hosted a forum in Jinan to promote the ecological protection and high-quality development of the Yellow River Basin and delivered an important speech. He stressed the need to scientifically analyze the current situation of ecological protection and high-quality development of the Yellow River Basin and grasp the major issues of promoting ecological protection and high-quality development of the Yellow River Basin. The Chinese people should adhere to the goal, down-to-earth, head-down, unremitting, to ensure that the "14th Five-Year" period of the Yellow River Basin ecological protection

and high-quality development to achieve significant results. They should strive unremittingly, so that the Yellow River will always benefit the Chinese nation.

From March 2020 to May 2022, the leading group for ecological protection and high-quality development of the Yellow River Basin in Henan Province had held six meetings for debriefing and deployment so as to thoroughly study and implement the important speeches and instructions of General Secretary Xi Jinping on ecological protection and high-quality development of the Yellow River Basin, striving to "make the Yellow River a happy river for the people" and to ensure that the ecological protection and high-quality development of the Yellow River Basin continues to make new progress and achievements in Henan Province.

On January 19, 2022, Han Zheng, member of the CPC Central Committee Political Bureau Standing Committee, Vice Premier of the State Council, guiding group leader of promoting the ecological protection and high-quality development of the Yellow River Basin, presided over the plenary meeting to promote the ecological protection and high-quality development of the Yellow River Basin. Han Zheng pointed out that to promote the ecological protection and high-quality development of the Yellow River Basin, is the CPC Central Committee's major decision and deployment with Comrade Xi Jinping as the core. The Chinese people should firmly grasp the strategic direction of joint protection and joiht governance advanced in coordination, implement the principle of "managing the city, the land, the people and the production based on water conditions", the land by water, the people by water and the production by water", always adhere to the problem-oriented principle, and promote the Yellow River Basin ecological protection and quality development.

At present, socialism with Chinese characteristics has entered a new era, and water management and water development ushered in a rare strategic new opportunity. General Secretary Xi Jinping pointed out that the focus of management of the Yellow River is on protection and regulation. The ecological protection and high-quality development of the Yellow River Basin has been upgraded to a national strategy, and the Yellow River Basin will move into a new stage of ecological protection and high-quality development. We should study and summarize the history of the Yellow River regulation of our

历史经验与理论支撑，以新时代治水工作重点为指导，传承弘扬黄河文化，优化水资源调配，打造人水和谐生态格局，加强流域生态保护，坚持水灾害治理，推动开创新时代黄河流域生态保护和高质量发展新局面。

面向未来，我们将按照《黄河流域生态保护和高质量发展规划纲要》的顶层设计，坚持以习近平新时代中国特色社会主义思想为指导，坚持以人民为中心的发展思想，准确把握重在保护、要在治理的战略要求，将黄河流域生态保护和高质量发展作为事关中华民族伟大复兴的千秋大计，统筹推进山水林田湖草沙综合治理、系统治理、源头治理，加强上游水源涵养能力建设，推进下游湿地保护和生态治理，加强全流域水资源节约集约利用，全力保障黄河长治久安，着力改善黄河流域生态环境，着力优化水资源配置，着力促进全流域高质量发展，着力改善人民群众生活，让黄河成为造福人民的幸福河。

predecessors, implement the new development concept and the new period of water management policy, provide historical experience and theoretical support for poverty alleviation and ecological civilization construction, take the new era of water management priorities as a guide, inherit and promote the Yellow River culture, optimize water resources allocation, create a harmonious ecological pattern of people and water, strengthen the ecological protection of the basin, adhere to water disaster management, and promote a new era of ecological protection and high-quality development of the Yellow River Basin.

Looking to the future, the Chinese people will follow the top-level design of The Yellow River Basin Ecological Protection and High-Quality Development Plan, adhere to Xi Jinping's thought of socialism with Chinese characteristics in the new era as a guide, adhere to the people-centered development thinking, accurately grasp the strategic requirements of the emphasis on protection and regulation. They should take the ecological protection and high-quality development of the Yellow River Basin as a great plan for the great rejuvenation of the Chinese nation. They should coordinate and promote the comprehensive management of mountains, water, forests, lakes, grasses and sand, system management, source management, strengthen the upstream water conservation capacity, promote the downstream wetland protection and ecological management. They should also strengthen the conservation and intensive use of water resources in the whole basin, and make every effort to protect the long-term stability of the Yellow River. And focus will be given on improving the ecological environment of the Yellow River Basin, optimizing the allocation of water resources, promoting the quality development of the whole basin, and improving people's lives, so that Yellow River will become a happy river for the benefit of the people.

四、气候变化与黄河流域生态保护

20世纪80年代以来,在全世界范围内极端气候频发、自然灾害频现,气候变化越来越影响着人类的生存和发展,全球气候治理已成为最受全世界瞩目、影响最为深远的议题之一。中国除了西北地区属于干燥的大陆性气候之外,大部分地区属于季风区。季风气候的变异性,导致中国降水及河川径流年内集中,年际变化大。作为中国重要的生态安全保护屏障,黄河流域在水源涵养、生物多样性保护、水土保持、调节气候等方面发挥着重要作用。近年来,在气候变化和人类活动的双重影响下,黄河流域生态环境问题突出,生态安全面临严峻挑战,主要体现在以下层面。

1. 气温演变:季节差别大,温差悬殊

早在19世纪70年代以前,黄河流域气温较为稳定。到了80年代,流域内气温开始呈现上升趋势。气温上升的速度在19世纪90年代以来显著提高,并且存在区域差异;全流域各季节的平均气温增速加快,其中冬季最为明显。新中国成立以来,黄河流域气候趋于暖干化。在全球变暖的大背景下,黄河流域的气候正在发生改变,近年来极端自然现象更为突出,如洪水、干旱、暴雨等。气候变暖严重影响了黄河流域水资源量的多少,进而影响了黄河流域生态系统格局。此外,黄河流域在快速城镇化、农业开发、退耕还林等人类活动及流域开发的影响下,出现了像土地沙化、局部断流等和湿地退化相关的生态问题。

IV. Climate Change and Ecological Conservation in the Yellow River Basin

Since the 1980s, climate change has increasingly affected the survival and development of mankind through the frequent occurrence of climate extremes and natural disasters around the world. Global climate regulation has become one of the most attention-grabbing and far-reaching issues in the world. Except for the dry continental climate in the northwest of China, most of the country belongs to the monsoon region. The variability of the monsoon climate leads to the concentration of precipitation and river runoff in China within the year and large inter-annual variations. As an important ecological security protection barrier in China, the Yellow River Basin plays an important role in water conservation, biodiversity protection, soil and water conservation, and climate regulation. In recent years, under the dual influence of climate change and human activities, the ecological environment of the Yellow River Basin has become prominent, and ecological security is facing serious challenges, mainly at the following levels.

1. Temperature Evolution: Large Seasonal Differences and Wide Temperature Differences

Back before the 1870s, temperatures in the Yellow River Basin were relatively stable. By the 1880s, temperatures in the basin began to show an increasing trend. The rate of temperature increase has increased significantly since the 1890s, and there are regional differences; the average temperature increases faster in all seasons across the basin, with the most pronounced in winter. Since the founding of the PRC, the climate of the Yellow River Basin has tended to be warm and dry. In the context of global warming, the climate of the Yellow River Basin is changing, and extreme natural phenomena have become more prominent in recent years, such as floods, droughts, and heavy rains. The warming climate has seriously affected the amount of water resources in the Yellow River Basin, which in turn has affected the ecosystem pattern of the Yellow River Basin. In addition, the Yellow River Basin is under the influence of human activities such as rapid urbanization, agricultural development, reforestation, and watershed development,

2. 降水演变：降水集中，分布不均

黄河流域大部分地区年降水量在200—650毫米，中上游南部和下游地区多于650毫米。尤其受地形影响较大的南界秦岭山脉北坡，其降水量一般可达700—1000毫米，而深居内陆的宁夏、内蒙古部分地区，其降水量却不足150毫米。降水量分布不均，南北降雨量之比大于5，这是中国其他河流所不及的。在降水量方面，黄河上游地区年降水具有明显的增加趋势，而中下游表现为明显的减少趋势。值得注意的是，新中国成立以来，黄河流域大部分地区降水集中度为增加趋势，尤其是中下游地区。这说明黄河流域的极端降水过程正趋于增多。黄河流域多年平均降水量不到500毫米，空间分布不均，黄河上游降水量增加，到了

郑州的黄河雪景（李庆明摄）

and ecological problems such as land sanding, partial cutoff, and other ecological problems related to wetland degradation have emerged.

2. Precipitation Evolution: Concentrated Precipitation and Uneven Distribution

The annual precipitation in most areas of the Yellow River Basin is between 200-650 mm, and more than 650 mm in the south of the middle and upper reaches and downstream areas. Especially the northern slope of Qinling Mountain Range, which is influenced by the topography, its precipitation can generally reach 700-1,000 mm, while the precipitation in Ningxia and Inner Mongolia, which are deep inland, is less than 150 mm. The distribution of precipitation is uneven, and the ratio of rainfall from south to north is greater than 5, which is inferior to other rivers in China. In terms of precipitation, the upper reaches of the Yellow River have an obvious trend of increasing annual precipitation, while the middle and lower reaches show an obvious trend of decreasing. It is noteworthy that since the founding of New China, the concentration of precipitation in most areas of the Yellow River Basin has shown an increasing trend, especially in the middle and lower reaches. This indicates that the extreme precipitation processes in the Yellow River Basin are tending to increase. The multi-year average precipitation in the Yellow River Basin is less than 500mm, and the spatial distribution is uneven. Precipitation increases in the upper reaches of the Yellow River and tends to decrease in Shanxi, Shaanxi and Henan. On the whole, the precipitation gradually increases from northwest to southeast, and the overall precipitation trend gradually decreases, most significantly in the middle reaches. Precipitation in the middle and lower reaches of the Yellow River is mainly concentrated in the summer (late July to early August each year). And precipitation from June to September accounts for about 70% of the year; precipitation from July to August duing the midsummer can account for more than 40% of the total annual precipitation. The basin is dry in winter and in spring, and rainy in summer and autumn, showing the climatic characteristics of "rain and heat in the same period". The rain and heat period with sufficient light, high temperature and abundant precipitation is a superior climate condition in the middle and lower reaches of the Yellow River in China, which is suitable for crop growth. In terms of seasonal

山西、陕西和河南境内则呈减少趋势。整体来看，降水量自西北向东南逐渐增加，总体降水量趋势逐渐减少，在中游最为显著。黄河中下游地区的降水主要集中在夏季（每年7月下旬至8月上旬），其中6—9月降水量占全年的70%左右；盛夏7—8月降水量可占全年降水总量的四成以上。流域冬干春旱，夏秋多雨，表现为"雨热同期"的气候特征。光照充足、高温、降水丰沛的雨热同期是中国黄河中下游地区优越的气候条件，适宜农作物生长。从季节分布看，冬季的降水量增加，春、夏和秋季的降水量都呈减少趋势，特别在秋季减少最为明显。

黄河流域能否成功应对气候变化带来的影响，是评价黄河流域生态保护和高质量发展的重要指标之一。沿黄地区要围绕水资源保护、能源开发利用等问题，共同抓好大保护，协同推进大治理。黄河流域应对气候变化的治理，是上下游、干支流、左右岸的跨省跨区域协同治理和系统治理。这对中国维护国际地位和全球影响力，弘扬"人类命运共同体"理念具有重要意义。

distribution, precipitation increases in winter, and decreases in spring, summer and autumn, especially in autumn.

Whether the Yellow River Basin can successfully cope with the impact of climate change is one of the important indicators to evaluate the ecological protection and high-quality development of the Yellow River Basin. Along the Yellow River area to focus on water resources protection, energy development and utilization and other issues, together to grasp the big protection, collaborate to promote the big governance. The regulation of the Yellow River Basin in response to climate change is a cross-provincial and cross-regional collaborative and systematic regulation of the upstream and downstream, mainstreams and tributaries, and both banks. This is important for China to maintain its international status and global influence, to promote the concept of "Community of Human Destiny".

五、黄河生态保护与修复对世界文明的影响

　　历史上，黄河流域灾害频发，尤其是水灾严重，黄河下游更是有"三年两决口，百年一改道"的说法，给沿黄地区的人民带来了深重灾难，中华民族始终在与黄河水害做斗争。新中国成立以来，党和国家领导人民在黄河的治理、开发和保护方面进行了艰辛探索和不懈努力，取得了举世瞩目的成就。党的十八大以来，以习近平同志为核心的党中央立足于生态文明建设全局，明确了"节水优先、空间均衡、系统治理、两手发力"的治水思路，黄河流域经济社会发展和百姓生活发生了很大的变化，水沙治理取得显著成效，生态环境持续明显向好，发展水平不断提升。

1. 为世界江河治理与保护提供中国范例

　　唐代诗人李白在《将进酒》中写道："君不见，黄河之水天上来，奔流到海不复回。"黄河自西向东源远流长，巨大的落差使得黄河水如从天而降，势不可当。但在20世纪，由于天然水资源贫乏、人类用水日益增多以及缺乏科学管理等原因，黄河干支流频繁发生断流现象。进入21世纪，随着黄河流域降水量有所增加、小浪底水利枢纽工程投入使用以及水量统一调度后，黄河至今实现了23年不断流，彻底改变了黄河流域断流频仍的局面，为世界江河治理与保护提供了"中国范例"。

V. The Impact of Ecological Protection and Restoration of the Yellow River on World Civilization

Historically, the Yellow River Basin is prone to disasters, especially serious floods, and the lower reaches of the Yellow River have the saying of "two breakthroughs every three years and one diversion every hundred years", which has brought serious disasters to the people along the Yellow River, and the Chinese people have always been fighting against the water damage of the Yellow River. Since the founding of the PRC, the CPC and the government have led the Chinese people to make painstaking exploration and unremitting efforts in the management, development and protection of the Yellow River, and have made world-renowned achievements. Since the 18th Party Congress, the CPC Central Committee, with Comrade Xi Jinping as the core, based on the overall situation of ecological civilization construction, clearly formulated the "water conservation priority, spatial balance, systematic management, two-handed efforts" of water management ideas, the Yellow River Basin economic and social development and people's lives have undergone great changes, water and sand management has achieved significant results, the ecological environment continues to improve significantly, the level of development continues to improve.

1. Providing Chinese Examples for World River Management and Protection

Li Bai, a poet of the Tang Dynasty, wrote in *Invitation to Wine*, "The Yellow River comes from the sky and flows to the sea." The Yellow River flows from the west to the east, and the huge drop makes the Yellow River water seem to fall from the sky without stop. However, in the 20th century, due to the poor natural water resources, increasing human water use and lack of scientific management, the Yellow River mainstream and tributaries frequently shut off. In the 21st century, with the increase of precipitation in the Yellow River Basin, the commissioning of Xiaolangdi Water Conservancy Hub Project and the unified scheduling of water, the Yellow River has achieved 23 years of non-stop flow, which has completely changed the

小浪底水利枢纽工程
Xiaolangdi Water Conservancy Hub Project

2. 培育流域生态保护理念，向世界弘扬黄河文化

加强黄河文化支撑，培育流域生态保护理念。文化是一个国家、一个民族的灵魂，在"四个自信"中，文化自信是更基础、更广泛、更深厚的自信，是更基本、更深沉、更持久的力量。习近平总书记在黄河流域生态保护和高质量发展座谈会上强调，黄河文化是中华文明的重要组成部分，是中华民族的根和魂。他提出，要推进黄河文化遗产的系统保护，深入挖掘黄河文化所蕴含的时代价值，讲好黄河故事，延续历史文脉，坚定文化自信，为实现中华民族伟大复兴的中国梦凝聚精神力量。黄河不仅是中华民族精神的重要标志，而且是中华民族坚定文化自信的重要根基。在黄河流域生态保护的过程中，要更加重视黄河文化，做好黄河文化的传承和弘扬工作。通过引导全流域形成生态保护的理念，保障黄河流域生态保护的成效长久持续，建立起科学、完善的黄河文化体系，向世界弘扬黄河文化。

situation of frequent interruptions in the Yellow River Basin and provided a "China example" for the world river management and protection.

2. Cultivating the Concept of Watershed Ecological Protection and Promoting the Yellow River Culture to the World

The Chinese people will strengthen the Yellow River cultural support, and cultivate the concept of ecological protection of the watershed. Culture is the soul of a country and a nation. In the "four self-confidences", cultural confidence is the more basic, broader and lasting confidence and power. General Secretary Xi Jinping stressed at the symposium on ecological protection and high-quality development of the Yellow River Basin, the Yellow River culture is an important part of Chinese civilization, and the root and soul of the Chinese nation. He proposed to promote the systematic protection of the Yellow River cultural heritage, to dig deeper into the value of Yellow River culture in the current era, to tell the story of the Yellow River, to continue the historical lineage, to firm cultural confidence, and to achieve the great rejuvenation of the Chinese nation's Chinese dream to gather spiritual strength. The Yellow River is not only an important symbol of the spirit of the Chinese nation, but also an important root of the Chinese nation's firm cultural self-confidence. In the process of ecological protection of the Yellow River Basin, the Chinese people will pay more attention to the Yellow River culture and do a good job of inheritance and promotion of the Yellow River culture. By guiding the formation of the concept of ecological protection in the whole basin, the Chinese people will ensure the effectiveness of the ecological protection of the Yellow River Basin in the long term, establish a scientific and sophisticated Yellow River cultural system, and promote the Yellow River culture to the world.

小浪底（董保华摄）

3. 彰显中国特色社会主义制度的优越性

黄河是中华民族的母亲河，也是全世界泥沙含量最高、治理难度最大、水害严重的河流之一。新中国成立后，在中国共产党的带领下，黄河变害为利。尤其是十八大以来，习近平总书记亲自到黄河流域考察调研，并做出一系列重要部署。2019年，习近平总书记主持召开座谈会，擘画黄河流域生态保护和高质量发展重大国家战略，发出了"让黄河成为造福人民的幸福河"的伟大号召，这也是新的历史条件下黄河治理战略的全面升级。该战略着眼于国家发展全局，面向社会主义现代化强国建设的未来，运用了系统治理、整体治理、协同治理的理论思维，是新时代治理黄河的宣言，彰显了中国社会主义制度的优越性。黄河安澜七十余年，是中国共产党治理能力的集中反映，得益于集中力量办大事

3. Highlighting the Superiority of the Socialist System with Chinese Characteristics

The Yellow River is the mother river of the Chinese nation. It also has the highest sediment content in the world. It is the most difficult to manage and one of the rivers where serious water damage occurs. After the founding of New China, under the leadership of the CPC, the Yellow River has been transformed from a harmful river into a beneficial one. In particular, since the 18th National Congress, General Secretary Xi Jinping has personally visited the Yellow River Basin for research and made a series of important arrangements. In 2019, General Secretary Xi Jinping hosted a symposium to draw a major national strategy for the ecological protection and high-quality development of the Yellow River Basin, issuing a great call to "make the Yellow River a happy river for the benefit of the people", which is a comprehensive upgrade of the Yellow River management strategy under new historical conditions. The strategy focuses on the overall development of the country and is oriented towards the future of building a strong socialist modern state. It applies the theoretical thinking of systematic, holistic and collaborative governance, and is a manifesto for the regulation of the Yellow River in a new era, highlighting the superiority of China's socialist system. Thanks to the system advantages of concentrating on doing great things, the Yellow River has been at peace for more than 70 years, which is a central reflection of the CPC's ability of governance.

The overall goal of the ecological protection and quality development of the Yellow River Basin is to fundamentally manage the Yellow River, to promote the historic transformation of the Mother River from a "worrying river" to a "happy river", and to realize the millennium dream of the Chinese nation. The development and introduction of The Outline of the Plan for the Ecological Protection and High-Quality Development of the Yellow River Basin particularly reflects of the CPC's commitment to the people and the historical leap in understanding the laws of Yellow River management. The Chinese people's cause of harnessing the Yellow River has stood at a new starting point with a general objective and a general outline for the new era.

In October 2016, Chen Run'er, then deputy secretary of the Henan Provincial Party Committee and governor, pointed out at a symposium to commemorate 70

的制度优势。

黄河流域生态保护和高质量发展,追求的总目标是从根本上治理黄河,推进母亲河从"忧患河"到"幸福河"的历史性转变,实现中华民族的千年梦想。尤其是《黄河流域生态保护和高质量发展规划纲要》的制定和出台,更是体现了中国共产党为民初心的接力传承,体现了对治黄规律认识的历史性跨越。人民治黄事业已经站在了新的起点上,有了新时代奋斗的总目标、总纲领。

2016年10月,时任河南省委副书记、省长陈润儿在纪念人民治理黄河70年座谈会上指出,河南省委、省政府一贯高度重视治黄工作,与黄河水利委员会密切配合、多管齐下、综合施策,促进了河南黄河治理与全流域治理有机结合、统筹推进。70年来,河南境内先后修建了一大批水利枢纽工程,完善了黄河水沙调控体系;开展游荡性河道的重点整治;实施最严格的水资源管理制度;大力实施引黄灌溉。

今后,中国在黄河治理开发新的进程中,要从实现中华民族伟大复兴和永续发展的高度出发,切实把"创新、协调、绿色、开放、共享"的发展理念融入治黄工作全过程和各方面,统筹上下游左右岸,统筹节水管水兴水,统筹治水治沙治滩,统筹防洪抗旱减淤,大力推进黄河治理体系与治理能力现代化。我们要在习近平生态文明思想的指导下,继续建设好黄河生态经济带,实现中华民族繁荣稳定发展。

years of the people's control of the Yellow River that the Henan Provincial Party Committee and provincial government had always attached great importance to the management of the Yellow River and worked closely with the Yellow River Water Conservancy Commission with a multi-pronged and comprehensive approach, which promotes the organic combination and integrated promotion of Henan's Yellow River control and basin-wide control. Over the past 70 years, Henan has built a large number of water conservancy hub projects, improving the Yellow River water and sand control system. And Henan carried out key improvement of wandering rivers, implemented the most stringent water resources management system, and vigorously implemented the Yellow River irrigation.

In the future, during the process of regulating and developing the Yellow River, China should proceed from achieving the great rejuvenation of the Chinese nation and sustainable development, and effectively integrate the concept of "innovative, coordinated, green, open and shared development" into the whole process and all aspects of the Yellow River management work. The Chinese people will vigorously promote the modernization of the Yellow River regulation system and governance capacity by coordinating the upstream and downstream and both banks, integrating conservation, management and development of water, controlling water, sand and beach, as well as harnessing flood, drought and silt. Under the guidance of Xi Jinping's thought on ecological civilization, the Chinese people will continue to build an ecological and economic belt of the Yellow River and achieve prosperity and stable development of the Chinese nation.

Appendix: A Brief Chronology of Chinese History

中国历史年代简表
A Brief Chronology of Chinese History

五帝时代 Period of the Five Legendary Rulers c. 2600 BC-c. 2070 BC	黄帝 Huangdi (Yellow Emperor)	
	颛顼 Zhuanxu	
	帝喾 Diku (Emperor Ku)	
	尧 Yao	
	舜 Shun	
夏 Xia Dynasty	c. 2070 BC-c. 1600 BC	
商 Shang Dynasty	c. 1600 BC-c. 1046 BC	
西周 Western Zhou Dynasty	c. 1046 BC-c. 771 BC	
东周 Eastern Zhou Dynasty 770 BC-256 BC	春秋 Spring and Autumn Period	770 BC-476 BC
	战国 Warring States Period	475 BC-221 BC
秦 Qin Dynasty	221 BC-206 BC	
汉 Han Dynasty 206 BC-220 AD	西汉 Western Han	206 BC-25 AD
	东汉 Eastern Han	25 AD-220 AD
三国 Three Kingdoms 220 AD-280 AD	魏 Wei	220 AD-265 AD
	蜀汉 Shu Han	221 AD-263 AD
	吴 Wu	222 AD-280 AD
晋 Jin Dynasty 265 AD-420 AD	西晋 Western Jin	265 AD-317 AD
	东晋 Eastern Jin	317 AD-420 AD

续表 Continued Table

南北朝 Southern and Northern Dynasties 420 AD-589 AD	南朝 Southern Dynasties	宋 Song	420 AD-479 AD
		齐 Qi	479 AD-502 AD
		梁 Liang	502 AD-557 AD
		陈 Chen	557 AD-589 AD
	北朝 Northern Dynasties	北魏 Northern Wei	386 AD-534 AD
		东魏 Eastern Wei	534 AD-550 AD
		北齐 Northern Qi	550 AD-577 AD
		西魏 Western Wei	535 AD-556 AD
		北周 Northern Zhou	557 AD-581 AD
隋 Sui Dynasty		581 AD-618 AD	
唐 Tang Dynasty		618 AD-907 AD	
五代十国 Five Dynasties and Ten States	五代 Five Dynasties 907 AD-960 AD	后梁 Later Liang	907 AD-923 AD
		后唐 Later Tang	923 AD-936 AD
		后晋 Later Jin	936 AD-947 AD
		后汉 Later Han	947 AD-950 AD
		后周 Later Zhou	951 AD-960 AD
	十国 Ten States 902 AD-979 AD	北汉 Northern Han	951 AD-979 AD
		吴 Wu	902 AD-937 AD
		吴越 Wuyue	907 AD-978 AD
		闽 Min	909 AD-945 AD
		南汉 Southern Han	917 AD-971 AD
		荆南（又称"南平"）Jingnan (Nanping)	924 AD-963 AD
		楚 Chu	927 AD-951 AD
		南唐 Southern Tang	937 AD-975 AD
		前蜀 Former Shu	907 AD-925 AD
		后蜀 Later Shu	934 AD-965 AD

续表 Continued Table

宋 Song Dynasty 960 AD-1279 AD	北宋 Northern Song	960 AD-1127 AD
	南宋 Southern Song	1127 AD-1279 AD
辽 Liao (契丹 Qidan/Khitan)	907 AD-1125 AD	
西夏 Xixia (Tangut)	1038 AD-1227 AD	
金 Jin	1115 AD-1234 AD	
元 Yuan Dynasty	1206 AD-1368 AD	
明 Ming Dynasty	1368 AD-1644 AD	
清 Qing Dynasty	1616 AD-1911 AD	
中华民国 Republic of China	1912 AD-1949 AD	
中华人民共和国 People's Republic of China	1949 AD-	